Praise for Chris McGoff and *The PRIMES* ...

"How many books have we read that talk about how to assess the need for change? There are dozens, and they always fall short of their promised intent: to give us the keys necessary to lead and drive successful transformation efforts. Chris McGoff's The PRIMES *fills that gap. I started working with Chris in my former position as the Administrator for E-Government and IT at the Office of Management and Budget, at which time the U.S. was ranked 36th in the world for providing web-based government services to its citizens. Using many of the PRIMES, we became a powerful, high performance team, building a team of over 2000 leaders in the public sector using e-government initiatives to drive a citizen-centered focus for government. The outcome: the U.S. ascended to first in the world in its delivery of federal services to taxpayers, businesses, and other nations."*

Mark Forman
First U.S. Administrator for E-government and Information Technology
Office of Management and Budget

*"*The PRIMES. *is a user's guide for taking on challenging transformations. ... I have seen firsthand how the fundamental truths outlined in* The PRIMES. *can make the impossible possible. Read* The PRIMES. *if you would like to look at difficult and complicated challenges through a different lens."*

Major General Craig Bambrough
(U.S. Army, Retired)

"Chris McGoff has scoured the world for the best back-of-the-napkin diagrams—those rough-penciled graphic maps to human and group relationships that smack you between the eyes and make you shout, 'Yes! That explains it!!' He's tested these "PRIMES" in the crucible of real-life consulting—and has the stories to prove it. Only Chris could have married vision and practice in this way, and given us such a readable guide to why life works."

Rushworth M. Kidder
President & Founder, Institute for Global Ethics
Author of How Good People Make Tough Choices
and Moral Courage

"Michael Doyle was an early innovator in the development and use of the thinking tools contained in Chris McGoff's, work, The PRIMES. *The book is a tribute to the wonderful creativity that Michael and Chris shared in their work together."*

Juli Betwee
Managing Partner, Pivot Point Partners

"In the final analysis, everything we try to accomplish in business, government, and in our community involves human beings. Chris's generous compilation of this set of universal truths in the form of The PRIMES *has proven invaluable time and again to me as I navigate the challenging task of encouraging collaboration among the human beings of the world."*

Tim Hurlebaus
Vice President, Consulting Services
CGI, Europe and Asia

"… Leaders … in the throes of changing, or, more important, transforming an organization … are involved in some of the most challenging events of their lives. So much so, that [they] can be measured by the scars of the experience versus the successes. Now that I have read The PRIMES, *my approach toward those monumental efforts would have been much different. This book has clearly outlined how an organization can succeed based upon the experience of others without suffering the pains of past efforts. … [If I were] given another chance at transforming an organization, Chris would be with me in spirit through the tattered pages that I would read and re-read as my roadmap! Anyone who has ever solved a problem on a napkin will love this book; it is how many problems are solved."*

Mo McGowan
Former Assistant Administrator for Security Operations,
Transportation Security Administration
U.S. Department of Homeland Security

"If you are interested in marginal incremental improvement and hearing feedback as to what you already know, hire a consultant. If you want to truly transform your business and personal life to a new level, read and live The PRIMES. *Chris McGoff is not simply 'denting the universe'; he is opening us up to an altogether new dimension."*

Nick Deluliis
Chief Operating Officer, CONSOL Energy Inc.

"What do the United Nations, the U.S. Department of Defense, the International Finance Corporation, and the World Bank have in common? When they ran into problems, they called Chris McGoff. Why? Solutions. They needed them. Chris showed them how to find them. Read his book and he'll do the same for you."

Larry Danner
Head of School, Washington Christian Academy
Educational Consultant

"Chris combines acute power of observation, profound understanding of and empathy for human behavior, clarity of thinking, creativity, and, perhaps most important, courage in this deceptively simple set of guiding principles. Spend some quiet time in self-reflection on each PRIME to identify those areas where you can grow as a person and as a leader."

Chris Smith
Chief Operating Officer
U.S. Green Building Council

"Determined to bring the best-quality health care to the poor in Kenya, I floundered, wondering where to start. The best thing that happened to me at that critical time was having the benefit of a few days of Chris's time. We did not know then that the new venture we called 'LiveWell Health Clinics' was designed and formulated around The PRIMES. Chris encouraged us to 'envision boldly,' build in integrity, and trust as core values, and declare with date-certain outcomes the transformation we were making. He freely shared his wisdom and helped us see with greater clarity the needs of our people, by talking to hundreds of potential customers. This approach is by far the best foundation we could have laid for our company. I am so pleased that Chris has now published all this wisdom in this book. I have tried and tested the wisdom of The PRIMES, with phenomenal results, and highly recommend it for one and all!"

Liza Kimbo
CEO, LiveWell Clinics, Kenya

"Chris McGoff has distilled the primary rules of the road for outstanding consulting work, in collaboration with a pioneer in facilitation, Michael Doyle. The PRIMES are clear, visually iconized, and pure gold as guides to organization transformation. They're the keystone 'apps' for change. Push back if you want something different."

David Sibbet
The Grove Consultants International

The PRIMES are powerful guidelines for making a big difference anywhere, in any way, any time... I will be referring to the book for years. The clarity and simplicity of the PRIMES make them comprehensible and uncomplicated to apply in any situation. The concepts and values offer a path to insight on a foundation of respect for every individual and the limitless potential of teams.

Mindy Goodfriend,
Entrepreneur, Strategist, Board of Directors, Women President's Organization

THE
PRIMES

HOW ANY GROUP CAN
SOLVE ANY PROBLEM

CHRIS McGOFF

THE
PRIMES
HOW ANY GROUP CAN SOLVE ANY PROBLEM
CHRIS McGOFF

ISBN: 978-1-929921-25-6 (Paperback)
       978-1-929921-20-1 (Electronic)

COVER DESIGN: Ellen Burns

INTERIOR DESIGN: Thomas Taylor

ILLUSTRATIONS: Jim Nuttle

Published by:

Victory Publishers
an imprint of
Morgan James Publishing
5 Penn Plaza 23rd Floor
New York City, New York 10001
Toll Free 800-485-4943
www.MorganJamesPublishing.com

THE
PRIMES

Chris McGoff (right) and Michael Doyle (left)

To Michael,
for living large,
and being generous and courageous

To Claire,
for encouraging me to live unreasonably

To designers of the future everywhere,
for giving me hope and purpose

ACKNOWLEDGMENTS

This book is a collection of the essential, most powerful insights I've gained through practical experience over the last 26 years, in professions as diverse as running a funeral home to supporting change initiatives in some of the biggest organizations on the planet. It isn't a comprehensive review or an exhaustive reference of what experts have written about complex problem solving and organizational transformation. Others have expressed many of the ideas shared in these pages more eloquently and certainly more comprehensively. I've included endnotes to reference sources that I've found uniquely and significantly valuable. I apologize to all whom a more diligent scholar would've cited.

The natural phenomena revealed in this book show up whenever people get together and attempt something big. These principles belong to the collective human experience. Any value I add is in assembling, ordering, and naming these universal phenomena—the "PRIMES."

I deeply acknowledge the influence and assistance of Tom Taylor, Marybeth Fraser, Dana Theus, Patrick Kane, Cristin Datch, Ellen Burns, Dennis Kane, Tom Wade, Marie France, John Miller, and the folks at Morgan James Publishing in the design and crafting of this book. We set out to make *The PRIMES* accessible and relevant to all but especially to emerging "Universe Denters."

I appreciate the countless readings by and constructive feedback from my children, Erin, Ryan, Brock, Carli, James, and Casey. The future is in capable hands. My wife, Claire, a gifted poet, encouraged clarity and brevity. Jim Nuttle and Deirdre Crowley made complex concepts into elegant illustrations. I will be forever grateful to Michael Doyle's wife, Juli Betwee, and to David Sibbet, Steve Lynott, and Kai Dosier, for letting me join their mischievous band of Universe Denters. My thanks go also to Rush Kidder for taking me beyond right-versus-wrong arguments to where the intractable, right-versus-right dilemmas are played out daily and managed brilliantly. I'm grateful to the staff and clients of The Clearing, Inc., who, outfitted with the PRIMES, stand relentlessly for possibility and who produce extraordinary outcomes for the organizations and communities they serve. Finally, thanks to William Powers and all of my colleagues and students at the University of Maryland Graduate School of Public Policy, who provide me invaluable opportunities to practice and learn.

CONTENTS

MY DECLARATION

The clear, crisp San Francisco skyline streamed in through the long windows of Casa La Vista one April evening in 2007. We were Change Agents, gathered on Treasure Island, to pay last respects to Michael Doyle, the consultant, entrepreneur, and master at "denting the Universe," whose efforts transformed organizations large and small. We considered him our mentor—our "silverback." We took turns telling stories about how Michael stood with us in pursuit of powerful, transformational outcomes all over the world and showed us how to have a whole lot of fun at the same time.

I told Michael's fellow admirers how much I was changed by partnering with him on adventures that took us into the realms of complex problem solving and organizational transformation. My fondest memories were of times when we got stuck … and inevitably we did. Whether our client was the United Nations, the U.S. Department of Defense, or any one of the world's industrial giants, some part of our agenda would jump the track. Out of frustration, one of us would grab a cocktail napkin or a scrap of paper— whatever was handy—and make a quick sketch to show what was going on and how to climb out of our conceptual hole. Some of those spontaneous drawings illuminated essential yet previously undistinguished truths about how people effect change, solve complex problems, and transform systems. Before his unexpected death, Michael and I had begun to catalog these insights. We wanted to name these bits of wisdom that reliably helped us unblock the way to change and transformation. And we wanted to share them with a broader community.

That evening on Treasure Island, I made my formal declaration. I promised those gathered at Michael's memorial service that I'd finish the job he and I started. I'd assemble our most powerful sketches in a book that was short, visual, and absorbed easily in chunks. There they'd be: our on-the-job epiphanies, offered to any and all who were up to something big. True, I knew very little about publishing a book, but I trusted that everything I needed was out there somewhere and would come to my rescue. The world showed up.

The PRIMES reveals universal patterns of human behavior and outfits you for effective leadership. The book you hold in your hands is the realization of my declaration.

For whom? You. Us.
When? Now.
Why? Because the world is waiting.

❧ Chris McGoff

PROLOGUE

THE PRIMES AND HOW THEY WERE REVEALED

"So what do you think?" The Director of Strategy for the World Bank Group, Christina Wallich, sat with a dozen or so typed pages spread out on her big, polished desk. It was the first time Michael Doyle and I had been inside the World Bank. Jumping out of a cab at the corner of 18th and I Streets in Washington, D.C., I noticed that the facade of the building looked like a gigantic spreadsheet, with block-long rows and columns of windows that extended 13 stories into the sky. Seven thousand extraordinarily intelligent people work at the World Bank's headquarters, including the highest concentration of PhDs in the city, and more than its share of renowned economists. Michael was one of my partners in a management consultancy I had founded a few years earlier. He paid the cabdriver, climbed out into the cool spring air, and shouted, "This is going to be so much fun!" I wasn't sure what was about to happen, but I'd heard that the World Bank had the best cafeteria in town.

Christina Wallich waited while Michael and I scanned the pages on her desk. They described a proposed design for the World Bank's soon-to-be-launched transformation process. The Bank was 50 years old and under intense pressure to change its ways. People were actually in the streets, chanting "50 years is enough!" The stakes were high. Michael and I had been called in after the Bank terminated its contract with one of the "Big Six" consulting firms. We were to review Christina's approach to one of the largest organizational transformations ever attempted.

I was a bit overwhelmed and wasn't quite sure what to say. Michael looked up from the documents, straight into Christina's eyes, and said, "It won't work."

Christina hesitated before she said, "That's my sense as well. That's why you're here and the people who designed this are not. But what specifically do you see wrong with this process?" Michael took a piece of scrap paper and made two quick sketches. He labeled one "Parity" and the other "Logic."

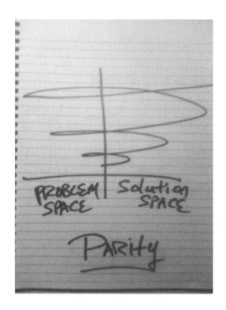

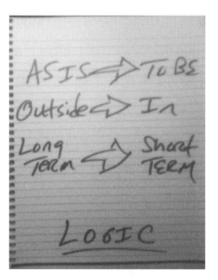

"First," Michael said, "this design won't work because it violates the 'Rule of Parity': People need approximately as much space to talk about the problem as they do the solution. The current design left far too little space for the senior leaders to really get clear on the problem and too much space for the solutions. The design violates the natural logic of group planning and collaboration. Groups work best when they start with the 'As Is' and then move to the 'To Be'," Michael explained. "They need to start by thinking about the world and their *outside* environment, and then consider what's going on in their organization. They need to start with their *long-term* plans and then move to their *short-term* plans." The current design had this all mixed up. "People will get lost," Michael said. "This process won't result in the outcomes you want and need."

Michael's little sketches, made in the heat of battle and just in time, enabled me to visualize and understand important principles that I didn't previously. Through the lens of PARITY and LOGIC, I could see how the proposal lacked balance and was illogical in its flow. If the plan were executed as it was designed, it was sure to add to the chaotic environment that the Bank's staff were already experiencing. Michael told Christina and me to redesign the process by following the PARITY and LOGIC principles, and everything would be fine. We did and it was. The president of the World Bank Group at the time was James Wolfensohn. He and his 100-person leadership team enthusiastically plunged into our redesigned process, which resulted in building a clear strategy to transform the World Bank. Over the next several years, I worked with the Bank to successfully implement the strategy. Since then, I've applied PARITY and LOGIC in dozens of large-scale projects and they've never failed me. They can't. They're simple, enduring, and universally applicable truths. They are what I call PRIMES.

I met Michael Doyle in 1989. I was doing research at IBM and developing "Groupware"—a precursor to "social media." I knew a lot about technology, but I needed to know more about how groups naturally worked, and the processes they used to collaborate and solve problems. Michael had coauthored a popular book, *How to Make Meetings Work*, and was considered an expert on consensus building, complex problem solving, change management, and organizational transformation. He and his associates had a long list of impressive achievements, including Ford Motor Company's design and production of the Taurus. They helped win citywide agreement to protect sightlines to the San Francisco Bay by forging a public policy consensus around building height restrictions. Michael helped the team that had propelled DuPont years ahead of the competition in developing and marketing an environmentally friendly alternative to ozone-destroying chlorofluorocarbon coolants. These were big problems, and Michael was always in the middle of their solutions.

Michael Doyle and his colleagues contributed greatly to our work at IBM. He recognized that it would be easy to develop computer technology to support the "anything goes" group process of idea generation and brainstorming. He observed that the real need and bigger challenge was to develop technology to help groups reduce their options to a single decision. Michael contended that the Holy Grail of technology-supported group work was a system that enabled decision making by large teams of people, who participated individually from different places and at different times.

Michael also helped our IBM team see that voting represented the lowest level of decision making and that it should be used only when all other collaboration processes failed. More than two decades later, the internet is clogged with idea generation, blogs, and voting tools. At the same time, little progress has been made to support the uniquely human experience of collaborative decision making.

Michael Doyle and his team had a deep and practical understanding of the true nature of group work. They knew how to unlock the power of a group and catalyze the social construction of knowledge. I watched them accomplish "something big" over and over again. I called them "Universe Denters."

The experience of working with Michael and his colleagues was thrilling. In my mid-thirties I was having the time of my life, yet I yearned for more. I started to think about getting more deeply involved with "transformational consultants," like Michael and his colleagues. I sensed a calling. For the first time since joining IBM 10 years earlier, wanderlust began to take hold of me. I talked about it with my wife, Claire, as we washed dishes one evening after dinner, while music played in the background and our three young children played on the floor. I said that I'd like to leave IBM some day and start my own consulting business. Claire looked at me and asked, "Are you saying that you wouldn't like to work at IBM through retirement at 60?"

"That, I'm sure of," I said. "I love the place, but I definitely want to try something else before I die. I just don't know when to make the break."

Without a pause, Claire said simply, "Jump now."

I was stunned, but her logic was pure. She said, "It's never going to be easier for us to take this risk than right now. We're as healthy as we'll ever be. The children are young, and their needs are small. If you're ever going to jump, jump now. It's only going to get harder the longer we wait, and I sure don't want to live with you regretting that we never took the plunge."

Three months later, without a regular paycheck, I joined "Universe Denters," who were gracious enough to let me in. Some friends and I launched an operation in Washington, D.C., which I hoped would be similar to Michael Doyle's on the West Coast, but with a greater emphasis on emerging technologies. Michael and I wound up as "partners in possibility." He brought a deep understanding of how teams naturally worked, and I brought the expertise needed to design and build computer technology to support the team process. Together we helped shape some of the early network-based systems that eventually led to what became known as "Web 2.0 Social Technologies."

In the process of scaling one organizational challenge or another, over a period of many years, realizations came to my partners and me one at a time—and often just in time. The PRIMES are these "eureka" insights. Usually, they occurred when we got stuck as a team. When something was wrong and we were in trouble, we talked it through. A realization would often surface that fit the exact circumstance and allowed us to move forward. As we refined and reused an insight successfully in other circumstances, we knew we had uncovered a PRIME. To qualify, the insight had to be universally applicable, effective in a wide variety of situations, and it had to be timeless and simple. One after another, we "met" the PRIMES.

This book describes the current inventory of 32 PRIMES.

DISTINGUISHING THE PRIMES

One of the most profound revelations in my life is that naming things is the act of creating the human experience and shaping the future. Naming is the core of what we do and what we cause. Naming is an essential first step toward achieving mastery over any aspect of life.

This is not a new idea. The first act between God and man was to name things. The ability to distinguish each thing by name was the essential first step for the first human to master, as he took dominion over the Earth.

> *And out of the ground the LORD God formed every beast of the field and every fowl of the air; and brought them unto Adam to see what he would call them: and whatsoever Adam called every living creature, that was the name thereof. And Adam gave names to all cattle, and to the fowl of the air, and to every beast of the field.*
>
> ✍ Genesis 2:19

The power of naming works deep in the human psyche. In 1882, an 18-month-old child was diagnosed with "brain fever." At the time, it was believed that the fever left its victim an "idiot." By the time she was seven, and understanding very little of the world around her, Helen Keller's wild, angry, antagonistic, and obstinate behavior seemed to confirm the old belief. In March 1887, Anne Sullivan walked into Helen's life and saw her, not as an idiot, but as someone whom the fever had left blind and deaf. Anne understood that the child's animal-like behavior arose from the fact that she had no words in her mind. Helen Keller couldn't distinguish anything from everything. Imagine that!

Sullivan held Keller's hand under water and spelled "W-A-T-E-R" in the other hand. She repeated this sequence over and over, faster and faster. Suddenly, Helen froze. Anne Sullivan later wrote, "You could see the understanding wash over and through Helen. She knew … that the symbols [I] had motioned in her hand 'meant' water." Excited and hungry for more, Helen began touching objects and demanding names. By that evening, Helen had learned 30 words. Anne Sullivan and Helen Keller became inseparable. Names were assigned; distinctions were created; human experience emerged. This former "idiot" went on to earn a bachelor's degree, cum laude, from Radcliffe College in 1904. She received honorary doctoral degrees from Temple and Harvard Universities; the Universities of Glasgow, Scotland; Berlin, Germany; Delhi, India; and the University of the Witwatersrand, Johannesburg, South Africa. She was also an honorary fellow of the Educational Institute of Scotland.

In the pages that follow, we'll name some of the phenomena you can expect to encounter along the path to solving complex problems and driving transformational outcomes. These PRIMES work when facing smaller challenges, too. You'll see them appear every time a group gets together to accomplish something they've never faced before. By naming these phenomena, we'll distinguish them. Once they're distinguished, you'll recognize them in real life. Once you recognize them, you can deal with them appropriately and increase your chances of success.

> *The beginning of wisdom is to call things by their right name.*
>
> ✎ Confucius

FIELD-TESTING THE PRIMES

If you've never had the privilege of operating a consulting company, I can tell you from firsthand experience that young people are the heart and soul of the organization. If you can recruit young people and make them relevant and worthy in the marketplace, you can create a thriving business.

My first challenge in building a new consulting company was to attract a young, bright workforce. My partners and I were amazed at how many young professionals showed up, eager for a piece of the action. They had a passion for playing full out, and they were willing to work long, hard hours. They wanted to be Universe Denters, so we hired them. This young workforce we attracted in 2004 was unique in my experience and ready to take on the world.

One summer afternoon in 2005, I sat across the table from Howard Gardner and Rushworth Kidder in the faculty dining hall at Harvard University. Rush is the founder of the Institute for Global Ethics and a good friend. He thought Dr. Gardner might help me better understand my young workforce. I wanted to know what they valued, what they looked for in a job, from an employer, and what motivated them. Howard Gardner was part of a team of researchers from Harvard, Stanford, and Claremont Graduate Universities, who, since 1995, had been investigating the concept of "good work" by professionals in many different fields. Over lunch, Dr. Gardner shared the results of his research.[1] I came away from that conversation with my own experience and impressions validated.

Today, young professionals define good work as personally meaningful, responding to the needs of the broader community, and producing excellent-quality outcomes. Unlike their baby boomer parents at the same age, they seem less driven by money and security, and more by a desire to make genuine and substantive contributions to local communities and the world. It was clear to me that our company's success stemmed from giving our young professionals an opportunity—a platform—to perform good work.

Our young workforce was energetic but relatively inexperienced. The next challenge was to equip them with unique skills and make them valuable to our clients. We outfitted our staff with insights embedded in the PRIMES. Then we connected them to leaders in the public and private sectors, who were at work on what we agreed was important and complex. We encouraged our young professionals to use the PRIMES to help clients drive successful outcomes. The results were impressive.

These courageous men and women went out and fought way above their weight class and posted significant achievements. These young professionals tackled significant problems and implemented effective solutions at federal, state, and local government levels. They helped make U.S. government services available online. They facilitated the modernization and transformation of the National Guard and other agencies in the Department of Defense. They assisted a major coal producer in transforming its culture into one that valued safety first, with zero tolerance for unsafe acts. They helped build a system for health care services that extended into rural Kenya. They affected a broad spectrum of enterprises in the United States and abroad within the pharmaceutical, health, manufacturing, mining, technology, and agricultural sectors, and among multilateral organizations, such as the United Nations, the World Bank, and the International Finance Corporation.

I'm continually impressed by how quickly our teams of consultants master the insights embedded in the PRIMES to direct change, facilitate transformation, and solve complex problems. I'm always inspired by their courage and persistence. More than anything, I'm grateful that they are this way.

I assure you that the PRIMES have passed rigorous field-testing. The problems we must solve today are technically and socially complex. The stakes are high, and the scope is wide. We face challenges in climate, education, energy, food, medicine, natural disasters, natural resources, poverty, religious conflict, security, terrorism, and war. Locally, schools need overhaul, city services need to be transformed, and large infrastructure projects must be completed efficiently. Despite the magnitude of these challenges, I still sleep at night. Every day, I witness properly outfitted people cut through the foolishness in our world to produce extraordinary outcomes. It can be done. It's being done.

OUTFITTING YOU AND YOUR FELLOW UNIVERSE DENTERS

My goal is to equip you to step up to whatever challenges you choose, enroll people to take a stand with you, and affect our world powerfully and positively. It's important that you learn to recognize, and decode, the human behaviors that often appear when groups take on big problems. Once you understand the root causes of what's blocking progress, you can address them positively and to great effect. The PRIMES will enable you to manage the challenges as they show up and even prevent their occurrence. Our world is full of possibilities and problems that need urgent attention. There isn't time to discover these essential truths—the PRIMES— by accident.

The purpose of this book is to offer you a distillation of the insights that my colleagues and I gained over years of trial and error—the illuminations that stared up at us from drawings on the backs of envelopes and cocktail napkins as we worked to change the world. Once you master the distinctions embodied in the PRIMES, you'll increase your skills in leadership, driving transformation, and problem solving. You'll be able to see things that others miss and anticipate things before they happen. You and those whom you enroll will be outfitted to meet any challenge and produce extraordinary results. With The PRIMES in your pocket, you'll dent the Universe.

GETTING THE MOST OUT OF THIS BOOK

Certain phenomena show up when solving complex problems in any area of life, whether leading a team up a mountain, managing change in business, or transforming organizations. Keep a few things in mind as you read this book:

1. Enjoy the journey but keep in mind that, in real life, PRIMES show up in no particular order.

2. Be ready for the shock of recognition when a PRIME jumps off the page, confirming what you have long felt was true but could never quite articulate. Don't let it trouble you if other PRIMES don't "click" immediately. PRIMES will reveal themselves as you encounter the problem-solving terrain where they apply.

3. Skip around, if you like. Keep the book handy. Peruse it from time to time, because the relevance of specific PRIMES is likely to shift as circumstances evolve.

4. Share this book and other resources, such as www.thePRIMES.com. The more members of your team who are familiar with the PRIMES, the better your chances of meeting challenges together.

5. Finally, get a sketchpad, a 5mm mechanical pencil with 2B lead, and start drawing your favorite PRIMES. Listen to your inner voice as you consider each one. My hope is for you to become comfortable with the PRIMES and integrate them into your fabric, sketching each from memory, whenever and however the need arises.

Here's an overview of our quest to create the future, produce extraordinary results, and make a dent in the Universe:

PART 1:

We pay attention to our "calling" and our desire to make a significant, lasting contribution to organizations, communities, and society. The PRIMES in Part One will help us prepare to meet challenges and enroll others in our vision.

PART 2:

As we set out on our adventure, specific PRIMES help sustain us as a group. We'll discover PRIMES for beginning our journey and for dealing with inevitable dangers on the path. Other PRIMES will help us "see around the corner," to predict specific threats to our goal, and help us manage risks.

PART 3:

Our goal is near, but at this stage we encounter the greatest fatigue. Our best and worst behaviors begin to manifest themselves. We'll uncover PRIMES to help us protect the integrity of the expedition.

EPILOGUE:

We have achieved what we declared, and we stand at the top of the world. Here we enjoy the view, reflect on what we've learned, and chart our next adventure.

Now, let's get outfitted to dent the Universe.

Success is focusing the full power of all you are on what you have a burning desire to achieve.

ᔐ Wilfred Peterson

PART 1:

THE CALLING

Universe Denters feel a constant tug, a calling that urges them to take on the biggest challenges and step up to the most difficult problems—the ones no one else has conquered. These big problems can be overwhelming and frightening, even to the most brave among us. There is no guarantee of success. Even in the best of circumstances, with access to the most modern tools, a great reservoir of knowledge, and personal fortitude, there will always be risk. When we add foreknowledge and predictability to the resources at our disposal, risk declines and confidence rises exponentially.

No matter how uncertain the road ahead, the PRIMES map a trail to whatever destination beckons. They also challenge you to answer the call, by giving you reliable tools to overcome the fear and eliminate any excuse that may tempt you not to answer. When faced with great uncertainty, heed the things that are certain.

We make our plans. We step out, and then the world shows up in unexpected ways.

The reasonable man adapts himself to the world; the unreasonable one persists in trying to adapt the world to himself. Therefore all progress depends on the unreasonable man.

ᔐ George Bernard Shaw

CHAPTER 1

WANDERLUST

Very few know how to tap the power and creativity of a group of inspired people, but the simplest approach is also the most powerful. Once a shared vision is identified, a path opens for people to follow, which enables them to naturally focus their energy on the realization of a greater goal. The future of the world hinges on the Universe Denters, who have the imagination to envision what the world needs now and who know how to enlist others in the challenge to achieve what they can foresee. They step up to solve today's challenges, and anticipate and prepare for tomorrow's. They're changing and transforming organizations and systems around the world right now. Others are joining them, as more people say, "I no longer choose to accept things as they are. I can't ignore the calling to co-create our future."

Everyone is affected by the rumblings of our world as it changes rapidly in astonishing ways. While some may be frightened, huddled indoors to avoid what is, Universe Denters are already out the door, running toward new summits where challenges await. They're the first to grapple with new realities and help design new paths into the future. They're curious and even hopeful about where these changes are taking us.

Wanderlust comes from the German word, *"wandernlust,"* meaning to hike *(wandern)* to a new, desired place *(lust)*. Wanderlust lies within each of us. Some let it control their lives, while others try to ignore it or, perhaps, never feel it.

Whether you're on the trail to the summit of new solutions and possibilities, or just beginning to step out, I applaud you and stand ready to dent the Universe with you. I ask only one thing: to go beyond "trying." Let's declare which peak we'll summit and when, and be willing to live unreasonably to fulfill our declaration. This kind of living is powerful ... and it's intoxicating. All progress depends on it.

There is significant risk. Universe Denters encounter large and unfamiliar forces. Among the few who choose to go first, only some are outfitted with what they need to succeed, or even to survive the journey. The PRIMES increase your chances of success.

The five PRIMES in the first chapter will outfit you for the adventures ahead. They'll help you clarify your purpose and prepare you to let the world know your vision.

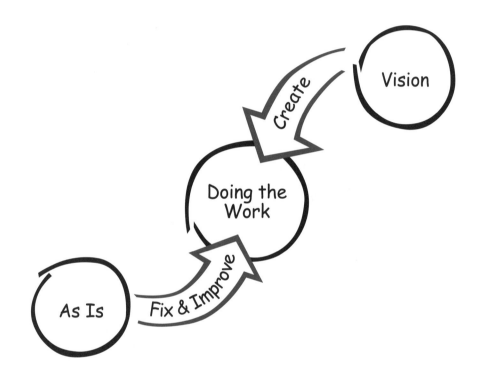

CHANGE VS. TRANSFORMATION

CHANGE VS. TRANSFORMATION

Change fixes the past. Transformation creates the future.
They aren't the same. Are you fixing or creating?

The chances of getting what we want increase as we become clearer about what we want. This is the fundamental power that underlies goal setting. To declare effective goals, we must first eliminate confusion between the concepts of CHANGE and TRANSFORMATION. To know the difference will help us recognize the fork in the trail that too many don't see. The two paths before us, one toward CHANGE and the other toward TRANSFORMATION, are both difficult. They have unique rewards; they lead to different summits and they produce different outcomes.

CHANGE requires us to become familiar with the current situation, and to work to make things better, faster, cheaper, or some other "er" word. The past is the fundamental reference point and actions are intended to alter what already happened. Success is judged by efficiencies and economies that are realized at the end of our effort, compared with when we started. When we choose change, our future is really a reconditioned or improved version of the past.

TRANSFORMATION is an assertion that "the future is largely subject to [our] creation."[2] The future can be described and realized when we free ourselves from constraints of the past. In transformation, we design our future and invent ways to bring it about. Transformation doesn't describe our future by referencing the past (better, faster, or cheaper); it births a future that is entirely new.

Like change, transformation also begins with firmly grasping the current state of affairs—the As Is. Without an intimate understanding of our As Is, we're delusional about the future from the outset. When we choose the path of transformation, it becomes easier to leave the past behind after we thoroughly consider the As Is. We permit ourselves to envision the future freely; we make specific promises, with full integrity, about how things shall be. We take action to ensure that we live into our declarations about the future.

In change mode, the desire to improve the past directs what we do. The past sets boundaries and constrains possibilities. Change is about making the system better. In transformation mode, the future directs our actions and only the limits of imagination and courage constrain possibilities. Transformation is about causing a new system to emerge. A butterfly is a transformation, not a better caterpillar.[3]

Transformation is the only way that a man landed on the Moon. In 1961, America and the Soviet Union played a game of one-upmanship. The Soviets had Sputnik and the Americans had Gemini rockets in competition to go around the Earth faster, better, and longer. That same year, President John F. Kennedy declared, "… this nation should commit itself to achieving the goal, before this decade is out, of landing a man on the Moon and returning him safely to the Earth."[4] Engineers were clear that no improvements to Gemini would realize this vision, so they invented Apollo. The Apollo space program wasn't a better Gemini but a unique system created in response to President Kennedy's declaration that an American would go to the Moon and back by the end of the decade. His declaration had all the necessary components of a transformation:

•   Crystal clear objective

•   Specific outcome

•   Certain date

From that declaration a new world was created.

The people you lead are doing something in the only time that exists: right now. The future hasn't happened, and the past is complete. The key question is, "What determines what they're doing right now?" Is it making a better, faster, cheaper past? Is it a commitment to fulfill a declaration and create a future? Is it the past or the future that drives the people you lead? It's one or the other but never both. Ignore this distinction at your peril.

Each path has unique hazards and challenges, and requires unique tools. Tools of change are embodied in corporate programs like Total Quality Management,[5] Activity Based Costing,[6] Six Sigma,[7] and others. All take the same approach: dismantle the existing system, identify the broken part, and fix it. These tools are effective when a better past is the desired outcome, but they're dead weight in the business of transformation. The instruments of transformation are imagination, declaration, invention, and innovation; they require a childlike fascination with "mashing" things together to create something new.

We elect leaders because they promise change. Yet issues like health care, energy, climate, and security cry out for transformation. When things don't work out, it's because we're on the wrong trail.

Notice the people around you: are they working to fix the past or fulfill a declaration about the future? Are they aware there's a difference? CHANGE is the right path when a problem is relatively simple, and the current system needs only a tune-up. TRANSFORMATION is the right path when problems are "wicked"[8] and a completely new system is required. Mastery begins by choosing the right path.

Many choose change even when they recognize that transformation is necessary. My experience shows me that these people carry a limiting belief, which tells them that powerful declarations don't work without precise clarity—the ability to see the future in detail. I'm persuaded that such clarity is not necessary, only clarity of intention. The PRIMES illustrate this truth.

This book is the result of TRANSFORMATION. In my past, I was never an author, and I had no reason to think of myself as one in the future. At Michael Doyle's memorial service, I announced my intention to write and publish *The PRIMES*. After Michael's unexpected death, my friends and I risked losing great wisdom about the best ways for groups to tackle tough challenges. I chose not to let that happen. To follow through on my declaration, I interviewed leaders and change agents all over the world. I learned what I needed to write this book. I lived into the transformation. For better or worse, I'm now an author. Mine isn't an improved past but a newly created future.

> *We shall require a substantially new manner of thinking if mankind is to survive.*
>
> ✎   Albert Einstein

The next three PRIMES are closely related to CHANGE VS. TRANSFORMATION. Transformational declarations must be made with integrity. They don't need to be fully baked, but you must risk believing that you can declare beyond your understanding of "how to," and you must trust the Universe.

INTEGRITY

INTEGRITY

Say what you will do and do what you say ... always.
What does your "yes" mean?

When I declared that I'd write this book, I also vowed to do so with INTEGRITY, by which I meant, "I say what I do, and I do what I say." To fully appreciate the value of INTEGRITY, it's paramount to leave aside all other connotations of the word. This PRIME isn't based on value, morality, or intention. It's based on action. When people choose to operate in INTEGRITY, their words literally create the world. They reach a level of performance that otherwise would be unattainable. Unkept promises are not merely empty; they're destructive and alienate every person whom we have labored to enroll.

Choosing to live in INTEGRITY is the greatest commitment a leader can make and is essential to produce extraordinary results. It's also difficult to accomplish, because such a pledge makes us vulnerable to scrutiny, not to mention failure, according to standards that may seem impossible to uphold.

Try it today. Simply be your word in all matters and observe the results.

Simply let your "Yes" be "Yes," and your "No," "No."
        ∾   Matthew 5:37

Most good leaders want to be perceived as approachable, involved, and respectful of people's ideas and requests. The temptation to say "yes" can be overwhelming and to say "no" seems counterintuitive. Even when you wish you could say "yes," learn to say "no" when there's no way to be certain that you can fulfill a commitment. Continue to say "yes" to everyone, and you'll discover that people care more about whether you keep your word than whether you're approachable. Learn to say "yes" only when you mean it.

Perhaps no other PRIME evokes such a visceral response in the teams I work with than INTEGRITY. Typically, I ask people if they're willing to be their word in all matters during the course of a project or activity. There are no small or big promises; there are only promises. When you make this commitment, you'll behave so that others can depend on you. Do what you say when you say you'll do it.

> *The most important persuasion tool you have in your entire arsenal is integrity.*
>
> ❧   Zig Ziglar

I'm no longer surprised by how much the invitation to live with INTEGRITY terrifies people. It's not easy to be our word, but what's the alternative? Do you want to scale an exposed cliff, with the person on the other end of your rope watching out for you ... sometimes ... maybe? Do you want to be involved in a project where deadlines become "guidelines" and meetings start "around" nine o'clock?

Universe denting is best attempted with those we can trust and who can trust us. Trust is essential for high-performance teams at work on a serious project.

INTEGRITY generates trust. When promises are kept, the reservoir of trust fills and is secure behind the dam of INTEGRITY. When promises are not kept, the dam is breached, the reservoir is drained, and it's difficult to fill again.

Learn to listen to someone's request and be aware as you choose one of three possible answers: "yes," "no," or "maybe." Be your word. Yes means yes. There are no exceptions or excuses.

> *Integrity can be neither lost nor concealed nor faked nor quenched nor artificially come by nor outlived, nor, I believe, in the long run, denied.*
>
>   Eudora Welty

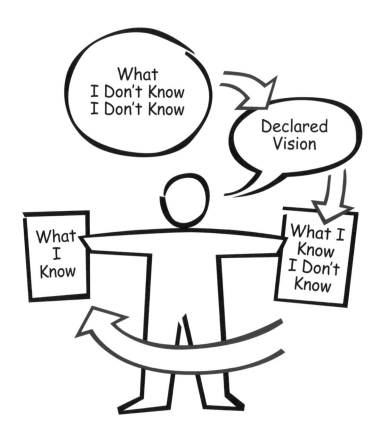

TRUST THE UNIVERSE

TRUST THE UNIVERSE

The universe helps people who live boldly. What happens if your heart creates visions that your brain doesn't yet know how to achieve?

Most people and organizations don't take time to create transformational visions. I know I don't always do it. I was struggling to complete this book until someone told me to imagine how fantastic I'd feel to have it done. She encouraged me to envision what life as an author might be like. Immediately, I saw myself in all black clothes, with facial hair, at a loft party in New York, surrounded by interesting people.

The point of this PRIME is that most people envision only to the limits of what they know how to achieve. When they limit themselves this way, they miss the fact that they can't possibly know all the resources the Universe has to bring to their aid. Because they're not looking for the answers, they don't find them.

Envision boldly. As you make your declaration, the Universe reveals everything needed to achieve it. Visualize beyond what you know.

In 1962, Americans didn't know what they didn't know about fulfilling Kennedy's declaration to land a man on the Moon and return him safely to Earth. The declaration itself caused everything to move from "not knowing we didn't know," through "knowing we didn't know," and finally to "knowing what we needed to know."

When you try to pick out anything by itself, we find it hitched to everything else in the Universe.

             ✎   John Muir

There's also a dark side to TRUST THE UNIVERSE. When I interviewed leaders for this book, I introduced the PRIMES to them as cards laid out on a table, with one PRIME on each card. I invited them to select four or five that particularly impressed them.

Dennis Whittle is a brilliant thinker, and we've traversed some serious inclines together over the years. Dennis quickly selected five PRIMES and gave me his thoughts on the first four. With the last card still in his hand, he hesitated and began to tap it on the table, a bit too hard. His eyes welled up, which is uncharacteristic of him. He held up the TRUST THE UNIVERSE card and said, "This one is schlock!" I knew more was coming, so I stayed quiet. "TRUST THE UNIVERSE is a myth," he continued. "It's a required myth, an *essential* myth for any true leader, but a myth just the same. Embracing this PRIME is the only real way to create transformative possibilities."

"Every leader better get this," Dennis said. "Only sometimes, after you make your bold declaration, you have to take out a second mortgage while you wait for the Universe to show up. And sometimes, not only does the Universe not show up, you lose your house. For every change agent entrepreneur with the Midas touch, for every tale of glory, there are a hundred stories of 'everything ventured, nothing gained.'"

The truth about TRUST THE UNIVERSE is there's no guarantee of success, no matter how bold or noble the declaration. People do get hurt. They risk everything, and some lose everything, every day. There are no secret codes, and every revolutionary leader, who stands up to regale an audience with "The Formula" for unfettered success, does so in retrospect.

We didn't land on the Moon without crashing a few rockets. Great leaders agree that failure often provides the most important elements for success. TRUST THE UNIVERSE provides the awareness to notice what your declaration brings, as though it were just sitting there waiting for you to discover it.

I met Dennis Whittle and his wife, Mari, in the late 1990s at the World Bank. We partnered to design and implement a new mechanism to promote innovation and microfinancing for entrepreneurs in developing nations. What started as a carnival of innovation became the "Development Marketplace."[9] Over a decade later, it continues to be an efficient mechanism, connecting social entrepreneurs rapidly to the resources of the World Bank. Dennis and Mari went on to found Global Giving.[10] This cutting edge, vitally important web-based alternative to traditional, multilateral institutions delivers investment funds to social entrepreneurs in developing nations.

TRUST THE UNIVERSE isn't about finding faith and being assured of success. Without a doubt, there are people who put no stock in the Universe and have achieved positions of wealth and notoriety. For a leader, however, to ignore Providence and all its potential is foolish. Great leaders struggle with the same challenges, frustrations, doubts, setbacks, and humiliations as everyone else. Leaders understand that, although TRUST THE UNIVERSE holds no guarantees, it makes it possible to get up every morning, start every day, imagine every possibility, create every vision, and, sometimes, achieve the unimaginable.

There are mixed reviews about how the Universe interacts with humans engaged in transformative and innovative endeavors. Consensus is unanimous on one fact: if the Universe doesn't engage with you, whatever you do won't matter; therefore, TRUST THE UNIVERSE is a prerequisite to any big leap. Ventures will fail, leaders will fall, and people will get hurt. Nevertheless, people will live, leaders will rise, and new ventures will take root, even as the aftershocks of previous failures continue.

In the beginning of the book, I acknowledged people without whose help I'd never have completed *The PRIMES*. Before I made my declaration to publish this work, I didn't even know that some of them were out there. *Thank you, Universe!*

Until one is committed there is hesitancy, the chance to draw back, always ineffectiveness. Concerning all acts of initiative (and creation), there is one elementary truth the ignorance of which kills countless ideas and splendid plans: that the moment one definitely commits oneself the providence moves too. A whole stream of events issues from the decision, raising in one's favor all manner of unforeseen incidents, meetings and material assistance, which no man could have dreamt would come his way. I learned a deep respect for one of Goethe's couplets: 'Whatever you can do or dream you can, begin it. Boldness has genius, power, and magic in it!'

                                                 W. H. Murray

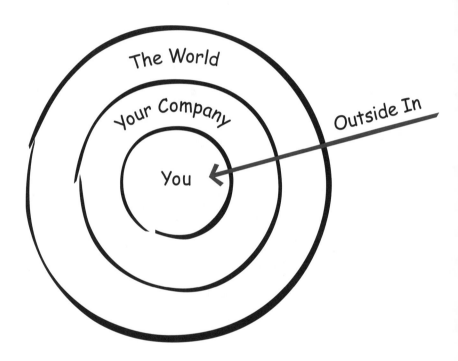

ENNOBLEMENT

ENNOBLEMENT

*Great visions elevate people in degree, excellence, and respect. Does your
vision touch people deeply and inspire them to act?*

Ennobled is the feeling of knowing we're part of something big and
important. A culture that embodies a deep sense of ENNOBLEMENT
inspires people to live boldly in pursuit of extraordinary outcomes. The
Apollo launch team understood that they were about much more than going
to the Moon. They knew they represented a great experiment of democracy
and freedom, in competition with communism. They were building a
complicated rocket, so that …

> … an American could be the first to land on the Moon, so that …

> … the world behind the Iron Curtain would have proof that freedom
> in a democracy was a better way to live.

During the years of the Apollo program, Americans shared a compelling
vision to stand on the Moon, and possibilities were abundant. Vision is a
terrific source of ENNOBLEMENT. A vision that ennobles and empowers
people makes clear what their world will be like, and what you and your team
will do to make it happen.

Creating a "vision statement" to foster ENNOBLEMENT is a mistake. A vision statement is a reductive thought about an expansive idea. While written statements can convey the essence of a vision to some extent, an ennobling vision is so expansive, rich, and textured that it can actually crowd out reality. Don't limit yourself to words.

How do we build visions that ennoble and empower people? Start with the fact that the ennobling vision must be larger than you, your team, or even your organization. Let's use the illustration of the ENNOBLEMENT PRIME:

1. Ask questions and find a vision that motivates you and your team.

2. Begin on the outer ring by describing the world you intend to create.

3. Describe how your team will be in that world.

4. Describe how you will serve the envisioned world.

5. Imagine what you and your organization need to do to make the vision real.

Powerful visions ennoble. They answer the question, "What do I stand for?" They provide direction when the way forward is unclear. They create a context for daily activities and lend meaning to every process encompassed by the vision, no matter how menial or challenging. People don't become ennobled by building an organization for the organization's sake. They become ennobled when they see themselves as an essential part of a group of people who are up to something big and wonderful for their community and the world.

The power of ENNOBLEMENT can be seen in the following story:

An Irish priest was walking down a country road early on a misty morning. He heard them before he saw them through the fog. They were laborers from the village, and they sounded upset with each other. The workers were grumbling, already disheveled and dirty at this early hour. Bricks and broken bits of brick lay in piles around the workplace. The priest stopped and asked the men what they were doing, and the foreman replied, "Me and the boys are making bricks, Father—fast as we can. Can't really stop to talk, no disrespect, gotta make a lot of bricks." The priest bid them good work and continued on his walk.

Soon, through the fog, he began to hear another group. The sound of purpose in the voices was distinct. When the priest reached the team of workers, he saw the same sand and rocks and water but a very different operation. This one was tidy, with very little dirt. These workers were laboring no less than the others, but they were much more organized and moved much more smoothly. The man at the head of the line immediately noticed the priest and said, "Good morning." The priest asked what the men were doing.

The man replied, "Father, we're structural guys. We're building the support structure for walls. Right now we're making the bricks. We have to make them at a certain pace because another team is making the walls, and we have to keep pace."

The priest blessed their work and continued down the road. As he walked, he began to hear joyous singing. Drawn by the chorus, the priest picked up his step and rounded the corner. There he saw the same sand, the same rocks, the same water, but the worksite was immaculate, and the work being produced was perfect. In fact, you could cut a piece of paper on the edges of the neatly stacked bricks. The pace was extraordinary, but these workers showed little sign of exertion. The odd thing was that they kept looking up the hill and smiling. Intrigued, the priest tapped the closest worker on the shoulder and asked what was going on.

The man smiled. "We're church-building masons, Father. In this project, we're mixing the sand and water, and making the bricks that go to the wall builders to build a house of God. When we're done, our neighbors, our families, and our community will come here to worship. How many times do you get to build a house of God?"

The priest tarried for a bit to ponder what he'd seen. He realized that the only difference between the three crews was the vision each team had. The first crew saw themselves only as brick makers. The second team saw their work as part of a greater whole; that context created a more meaningful perspective and resulted in their desire to make quality products. The third group had adopted a grand vision; they made every brick integral to the outcome and of the highest quality.[11]

Tapping into the human desire to participate in something grand and meaningful sets free an almost miraculous power source that compels us to go beyond the limits we perceive today. If you waste this resource, you deny others the opportunity to accomplish amazing things.

> *Good actions ennoble us, and we are the sons of our deeds.*
>
>   ✤   Miguel de Cervantes

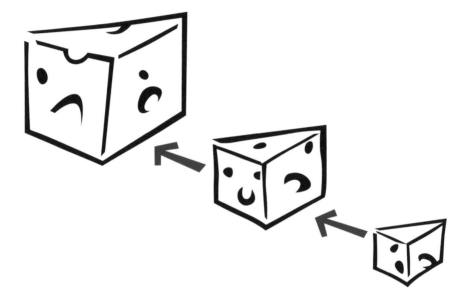

DYNAMIC INCOMPLETENESS

DYNAMIC INCOMPLETENESS

Great visions are delicious and full of holes
that invite others to taste and fill in.
Co-creation causes co-ownership.
Do you provide a clearing to co-create inspiring visions?

Transformational leadership and complex problem solving require the development of a clear, shared, and cogent vision. The worst leaders bring no vision. Almost as bad are the leaders who bring too much vision. The latter have ALL the answers about how things will be in the future. Their simple message is, "Follow me." Universe Denters, and Universe Denters in-the-making, aren't content to follow others; they're only motivated to contribute their talents by leaders who invite their creativity and ingenuity to the effort.

Great leaders bring just enough vision to move and inspire people. They present their vision and invite others to contribute their ideas to fill in the gaps. This process is called DYNAMIC INCOMPLETENESS. It is also known as "The Swiss Cheese Rule."

Think of a vision as a giant piece of Swiss cheese, delicious and full of holes. The leader's invitation to share the vision encourages others to plug the holes with more Swiss cheese by adding their contribution. Their actions, in turn, invite more people to plug other holes with more Swiss cheese. DYNAMIC

INCOMPLETENESS calls everyone to co-create the vision because there are always more holes to fill in. People develop a deep sense of ownership in what they help to create. Ownership is the first value of this PRIME. Ownership of the vision increases the probability of its success.

DYNAMIC INCOMPLETENESS recognizes that people resist completeness. The greatest visions are inspiring, ennobling, and empowering because they're incomplete. They touch people deeply and move them to say, "Yes, I'm inspired by what's here, and I can fill in some of the holes." This PRIME reveals the balance between the need for a leader to set out ideas about the future and to leave some things for the group to figure out.

> *"Would you tell me, please, which way I ought to go from here?"*
>
> *"That depends a great deal on where you want to get to," said the cat.*
>
> *"I don't much care where ... ," said Alice.*
>
> *"Then it doesn't matter which way you go," said the cat.*
>
>   ✎   Lewis Carroll, Alice in Wonderland

I've been asked many times why more leaders fail to offer their teams a vision. Every leader to whom I've posed the same question has expressed the same fear: to present an incomplete vision, without all the answers, might cause them to look foolish or intellectually incompetent. As DYNAMIC INCOMPLETENESS makes clear, however, they will not appear incapable. There's no need to have all the answers—it's impossible in any case. This PRIME offers reassurance: The candid leader is able to be collaborative and participatory. This PRIME reveals something further: Even if leaders did have all the answers, they would be unwise to provide them. "Not having all the answers" is the prerequisite for engaging people's energy in changing or transforming the system in which they've grown comfortable. It's also a terrific way to unburden leaders and reinvigorate them.

DYNAMIC INCOMPLETENESS challenges leaders to own their responsibility to share elements of the future about which they feel passionate. By pointing out where the vision is incomplete, they invite others to help fill it in. Leaders who adhere to this PRIME inspire loyalty and appreciation, since people contribute to the vision gladly.

> *The desire and pursuit of the whole is called love.*
> ଶ   Plato

John F. Kennedy didn't show blueprints of the Apollo spacecraft, describe the chemical compounds in rocket fuel, or talk about how to put peanut butter into a squeeze tube. He just said, "To the Moon and back." His declaration created DYNAMIC INCOMPLETENESS—a clearing for thousands of people to rush in with all kinds of new inventions and new ways to realize the vision. The world has never been the same.

DYNAMIC INCOMPLETENESS is a powerful way to TRUST THE UNIVERSE. What you don't know creates the invitation and the space for others to join you to bring forward information and ideas that you couldn't have imagined. As others invest in your vision, encourage them to follow your lead by filling in the holes with more Swiss cheese. As they engage in DYNAMIC INCOMPLETENESS with you, they'll fill in what they can and leave room for others to do the rest.

Let's review the five PRIMES described in this chapter:

- **CHANGE VS. TRANSFORMATION** helps us to be clear about what we're up to.

- **INTEGRITY** gives our words the power to create the world.

- **TRUST THE UNIVERSE** frees us to declare boldly.

- **ENNOBLEMENT** lends meaning to every activity encompassed by the vision.

- **DYNAMIC INCOMPLETENESS** inspires and invites others to contribute their insights and gifts.

In the next chapter, you'll be outfitted with five PRIMES to make sure you travel with committed and trusted allies.

> *Man is so made that when anything fires his soul, impossibilities vanish.*
>
> ✎   Jean de La Fontaine

CHAPTER 2

ENROLLMENT

Once you've answered the call, stepped up to a challenge, and declared to live in INTEGRITY, the first question should be, "Is there any way I can accomplish this right now by myself?" If the answer is "yes," do it. A competent person, who uses command and control decision making, can produce incredible results quickly —and should—if he or she can succeed alone.

If the answer to the first question is "no," the next question is, "Who needs to be enrolled and tied into the effort?" After decades of experimenting, I've learned to enroll a team no bigger than absolutely required and to outfit its members with only the essentials necessary to achieve the desired outcome in the shortest period of time. Every person you add to the team and everything you add to the process increases its complexity dramatically. Additional people also drive up costs and increase the risk of failure.

Consensus and collaboration are overrated, in my experience. Instead of thinking of them as aspirational values, consider them unavoidable necessities at certain times. When it comes to tackling big visions, it's wise to seek the counsel and enrollment of others. Usually, your outcome will depend on them. When the challenge you face necessitates the involvement of others, your capacity to inspire and enroll them will directly affect your ability to succeed.

I dare you to think bigger, to act bigger, and to be bigger.
I dare you to think creatively. I dare you to lead and
inspire others. I dare you to build character. I dare you
to share. And I promise you a richer and more exciting
life if you do!

ॐ   William Danforth

Fortunately, you will likely run into those who have been on a journey like yours already, who have scaled heights so great that they couldn't see the summit until they were on it.

The insights that follow will help you enroll others to share your vision. They will also allow you to appreciate fully the value of unity of purpose and solidarity of effort.

Never doubt that a small group of thoughtful committed citizens can change the world. Indeed, it is the only thing that ever has.

           ✎   Margaret Mead

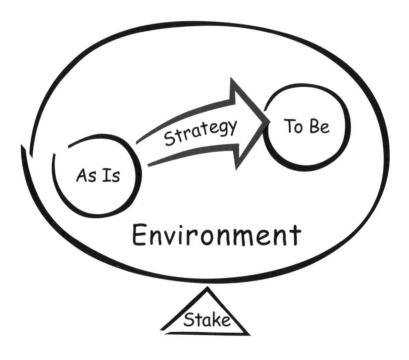

CORE PRIME

CORE PRIME

People in powerful organizations have forged essential agreements. How would you and your team members answer these questions:

What are you trying to achieve?
Where are you starting from?
Why is it important?
What must happen to be successful?

When achievement of your outcome compels you to enlist others, enrollment is an essential skill that you must employ to take people beyond mere compliance. They must be inspired by the possibilities of your vision, committed to the outcomes, and willing to act unreasonably, if necessary, to achieve them.

The CORE PRIME distinguishes five, essential agreements that enrolled people must maintain to achieve extraordinary results:

1. **ENVIRONMENT** — They must agree on what's happening around them, which they're unable to affect, but which will affect them.

2. **AS IS** — They must agree on the current situation as it really is.

3. **STAKE** — They must agree on what's at stake if they stay where they are and don't change.

4. **TO BE** — They must agree on a cogent vision of the future they desire.

5. **STRATEGY** — Finally, they must agree on how to break out of the As Is and chart an irreversible course toward the To Be.

The CORE PRIME is where everything begins and ends. It's immutable, and there's no room for interpretation. Remove one of the five agreements, and the whole thing falls apart. Not only is the CORE PRIME inflexible, it's the most often violated, and there's no learning curve. Get it right, you pass. Get it wrong, you fail.

The following are five conversations needed to implement the CORE PRIME. As you take in each one, ask yourself, "Doesn't this just make perfect sense?

CONVERSATION I
AS IS
— THE WAY THINGS ARE —

Before anyone will go along with you, they must believe in you. Your understanding of things as they actually are (as opposed to how you would like them to be) is the source of your credibility as a leader. Proof that you understand the current reality lies in your capacity to say, "This is how things are now," and for others to respond, "Yeah, that's how the situation looks to me as well."

Only by acceptance of the past, can you alter it.
                                    ꙩ   T. S. Eliot

Name and embrace it all: the good, the bad, and the ugly. If you try to shape perceptions or "spin" what's truly going on during this process, people may listen politely, but they'll walk away as soon as they can. People don't trust leaders who demonstrate a lack of appreciation for reality and who can't honestly acknowledge the way things really are. The As Is conversation is descriptive and fact-based. Its success emerges when the leader sets judgment and blame aside, which creates a clearing for people to offer their information and perspective without fear.

To state the obvious of the As Is seems like common sense, but it's something most leaders either fail to do authentically, or fail to do altogether. To demonstrate a deep comprehension of the world as it is creates the foundation for everything that follows. Eventually, the group will establish a collective sense of the As Is. To gain this agreement can be the most difficult part of the CORE PRIME.

CONVERSATION 2
ENVIRONMENT
— THINGS OUTSIDE OUR CONTROL —

This conversation identifies outside forces that can drive you forward or hold you back. These forces may surround you, yet they're beyond you; you have no control over them. The economy is an example of such a force. Most people would agree that nothing they do affects the economy directly. Used car dealers may see a "bad economy" as a positive, driving force, while real estate developers may see it as a restraining force. Individuals can change their company's future, they can change strategies, and they can change their vision. The economy, however, is outside the scope of what they can change. In the illustration of the CORE PRIME, the As Is, the To Be, and the Strategy float within the Environment. Environmental forces typically affect all three components, while many issues stem directly from the Environment. Major trends in employment, unemployment, and housing costs are examples of environmental forces, but whether they are in your CORE PRIME Environment depends entirely on where you sit. Individuals and companies may not be able to affect these trends directly. If you were the head of the Federal Reserve, however, these forces would be prominent in your As Is, as something over which you could exert direct influence.

To recognize what is beyond your control doesn't mean that you can ignore it. To ignore the Environment is like choosing a path to summit a mountain and disregarding the weather. After you prepare for the climb, pack the best gear, muster all your determination and commitment, you don't blow off the weather reports. You may not be able to control the weather, but it has the potential to exert enormous control over you; so much so, that if you ignore it, you may put your life at risk.

The question is, "Do you want to fight the Environment, or do you want to ride it?" Pay attention to forces beyond your control, and they'll carry you places you couldn't reach on your own. Ignore them and you may never know what hit you.

CONVERSATION 3
STAKE
— THE BURNING PLATFORM —

The Stake conversation represents "the fulcrum of possibility." Get it right and people tip toward the To Be. Get it wrong, or underinvest in it, and people tip back to what's familiar. They'll guard the status quo as if their lives depended on it. The Stake conversation answers the questions, "What happens when we succeed?" and, "What happens if we fail to drive toward the To Be and remain where we are, doing what we're doing?"

How many strategic plans end up gathering dust on bookshelves? How many times will a friend complain about his weight and pledge to get in shape but never do it? How many targeted reductions in greenhouse gases will we fail to achieve? Regardless of how much we complain about the As Is, and no matter how inspired we are by our To Be, nothing will happen until something we deem sufficiently significant is at Stake.

A powerful Stake makes the status quo seem more dangerous than a leap into the unknown. The Stake is at the heart of any effort to solve a problem, effect a change, or transform a system. Success literally rests on the Stake. Over the next few chapters, we'll answer the question, "What's at Stake?" You'll need the answers, not just to avoid negative consequences; you'll need them to let go of the status quo. If you don't let go, you'll miss the experience of achieving your vision.

CONVERSATION 4
TO BE
— WITHOUT VISION THE PEOPLE PERISH —
(Proverbs 29:18)

Ancient scripture doesn't say that the people *might* perish or that they *could* perish. It says they *perish*. Vision creates the context for every endeavor, every goal, and every moment committed to its achievement. In this conversation, people stand taller and speak with more deliberation; they grow confident, experience insight, and gain perspective. The To Be creates a reverence like that which many people felt when they heard Martin Luther King, Jr., declare, "I have a dream."[12] Every great leader is called to share a vision with which others literally fall in love. You don't create this vision alone, nor should you, even if you could.

We've already seen that the greatest visions are always incomplete and always emerging. Never fully detailed, the "holes" in the visions make them compelling; they are the voids that invite others into co-creation.

CONVERSATION 5
STRATEGY
— THE BRIDGE BETWEEN AS IS AND TO BE —

You've answered the call, presented your vision, and enrolled others in the quest. Your word—your INTEGRITY—depends on deciding the Strategy: who does what and when. Strategic planning often brings up negative connotations because it is frequently done without precision. After years of trial and error, Michael Doyle and I uncovered the essential principles of building and implementing a powerful Strategy.

The CORE PRIME shows that an effective Strategy rescues people from their current state and propels them into a compelling future, because the Stakes are so high.

When a Strategy is developed and presented, free-flowing anxiety over the gap between the past and the future is transformed into directed activity. This only happens when you focus on the fewest, most essential things that will alter the As Is. If your Strategy is insufficient to bring order to the energy created by change, chaos ensues and your process will spin out of control.

The Strategy resolves the intense, creative tension between authentically embracing the As Is—which the Stake revealed to be dangerous—and the ennobling vision of the To Be. There can be no "strategies." The word should never be made plural. At any given time, only one Strategy can be used to resolve the tension between what you have and what you want. The Strategy illuminates the essential actions you must take to realize your vision.

Omitting of one of the five conversations in the CORE PRIME doesn't leave the other four intact; it leaves zero, and your efforts fail. The goal of the preceding five conversations is to achieve and maintain agreement on the meaning of the following five items on which consensus is necessary for people to produce extraordinary results:

1.   The current situation they face;

2.   Environmental forces that drive as well as restrain them;

3.   Where they're going;

4.   What's at stake if they remain where they are, and what they'll do and have when they achieve the vision; and

5.   The fewest, essential initiatives that will dissolve the status quo and set the group on a course toward fulfilling the vision of the future in which they've enrolled.

The next several chapters will examine more deeply key aspects of the CORE PRIME. By mastering these insights, you'll find it easier to lead teams on large, risky, and exciting adventures.

When you are inspired by some great purpose, some extraordinary project, all your thoughts break their bonds: Your mind transcends limitations, your consciousness expands in every direction, and you find yourself in a new, great, and wonderful world. Dormant forces, faculties, and talents become alive, and you discover yourself to be a greater person by far than you ever dreamed yourself to be.

❧   Patanjali

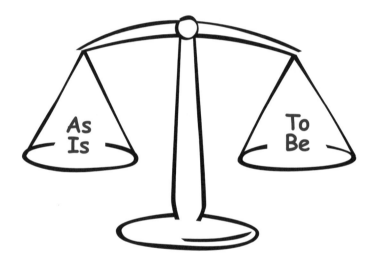

PARITY

PARITY

*Powerful visions balance authentic relationships
with what is and what is to be.
Do you spend more time analyzing the As Is
or imagining the To Be?*

The CORE PRIME revealed the conversations that must happen to enroll others to drive change and cause transformation. The PARITY PRIME reveals how to have those conversations.

PARITY means devoting equal attention and detail to each of the five conversations in the CORE PRIME. Overanalyzing the As Is and immediately attempting to build a high-level vision is unwise. Focusing on the As Is and the To Be, while giving only lip service to the STRATEGY and the STAKE, is equally shortsighted. PARITY's contribution to your success is keeping the level of detail proportionate across all five conversations and cycling through them each time there's a need to go deeper.

> *Rigor alone is paralytic death, imagination alone is insanity.*
>
> ⎄   Gregory Bateson

Groups can display different tendencies as they respond to the demand for PARITY. Here's how they play out:

ANALYSIS PARALYSIS

Groups characterized by Analysis Paralysis are most comfortable talking—or arguing—about the current situation, without ever discussing what's at Stake if they don't change. They're overly introspective, often uncomfortable with the idea of creating a vision, and may even feel they have no right to do so. To an outsider, these groups may sound like victims.

BLUE SKY

This term describes groups that are most comfortable when they dream about the future. Their characteristics are the opposite of those of Analysis Paralysis. Blue Sky groups find the status quo tedious and even embarrassing to discuss. They assume they understand the Stake when in fact they often don't. Unfortunately, their lack of attention to the As Is causes them to be ungrounded. To the outsider, they lack credibility and a secure sense of reality. Typically, the visions they develop fail to inspire people, including themselves.

BLUR

This kind of group is neither comfortable nor patient enough to drive agreement on the As Is, the To Be, or the Stake. They're made up of Type A personalities and have an almost intractable bias toward action. Members of groups characterized by Blur only want to perform "real work." Without agreement on the beginning and the end, however, their efforts are usually unfocused, inefficient, and ineffective.

BALANCE

A Balanced group is willing to go slow to go fast. Members take time to forge deep and comprehensive agreements between the stakeholders, across each element of the CORE PRIME. They adhere to the "cruel rule of reciprocity." The rule states that deep agreement on the As Is will elicit deep understanding of an inspiring To Be, and a deeply felt Stake will provide the impetus to take action. A detailed and cogent Strategy is all that remains to organize the activity.

More than a guideline, PARITY, like the CORE PRIME, is violated at your peril.

> *Not the autocracy of a single stubborn melody on the one hand, nor the anarchy of unchecked noise on the other. No, a delicate balance between the two; an enlightened freedom.*
>
> ✌   Johann Sebastian Bach

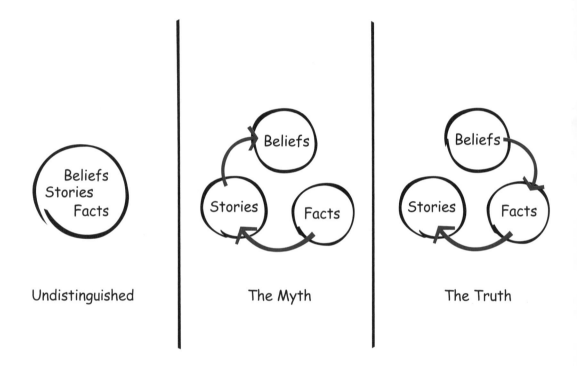

FACTS, STORIES, AND BELIEFS

FACTS, STORIES, AND BELIEFS

We put on our beliefs in the morning, and they shape
everything we perceive during the day.
What beliefs shape your perceptions?

Building the agreements embodied in the CORE PRIME requires substantial group discussions. The FACTS, STORIES, AND BELIEFS PRIME will outfit you with the awareness of critical nuances during these conversations, the skills to intervene, and the tools to keep the group on track. As a result, you'll help the group reach deep and binding agreements and make commitments to act on them.

FACTS, STORIES, AND BELIEFS are exchanged in any discussion, but many fail to make the distinction between them. As seen on the left side of the illustration of this PRIME, everything sounds the same and is treated the same. An example of the failure to distinguish FACTS, STORIES, AND BELIEFS may be found in the following:

> *"Our revenue was $50 million last year and that is*
> *simply not enough. Marketing is inept."*

The first sentence above contains FACT ("revenues were ..."), and STORY ("... not enough") to assign meaning to the FACT. The second sentence is clearly a BELIEF. In an undistinguished listening model, all three elements are treated as if they were equally true and important.

The center of the illustration shows "The Myth" some people accept once they learn to distinguish FACTS from STORIES and BELIEFS. They think we listen to FACTS ("Our revenues were $50 million"), interpret them, and form a STORY ("... and that is simply not enough.") From there it's easy enough to adopt the BELIEF that "Marketing is inept." Such formulations may be true at times; however, in complex problem solving and transformation, we see a different progression at work, which is revealed on the right side of the PRIME'S illustration.

> *The first principle is that you must not fool yourself, and*
> *you are the easiest person to fool.*
>   ᔍ   Richard P. Freeman

Quite often when people appear irrationally bogged down in an argument, the hidden truth that keeps them stuck is their failure to understand the BELIEFS that operate behind the FACTS and STORIES they're arguing about. People enter conversations with their BELIEFS well entrenched. Their BELIEFS create their reality, and they'll "shop" for FACTS to support the STORIES that reinforce their predetermined BELIEFS. The implications are substantial. When a group is fragmented and discordant, to debate the FACTS or to listen to STORIES is futile. More profit is gained by shifting the conversation to explore the underlying BELIEFS, and why they're held so deeply.

When BELIEFS are discussed deliberately and openly, they lose their hold on a group. Once BELIEFS are revealed, the group will naturally engage in a more productive discussion about FACTS and STORIES. Learn to distinguish FACTS from STORIES from BELIEFS.

> *He uses statistics as a drunken man uses lamp posts —*
> *for support rather than illumination.*
> ❧ Andrew Lang

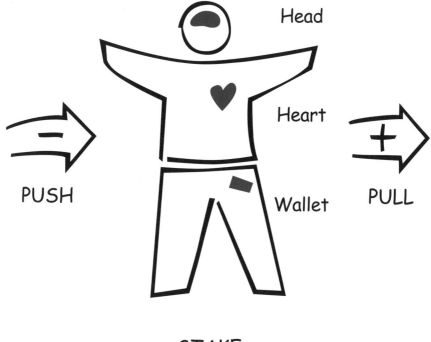

STAKE

Different people, different motivations.
Do you inspire the scientists, the poets, or the accountants?
Better yet, do you inspire them all?

The illustration of the CORE PRIME included a small triangle at the bottom, titled Stake. The STAKE fuels any effort to solve a problem, effect a change, or transform a system. Success literally rests on the STAKE. Over the past 25 years, my partners and I have seen the STAKE articulated both weakly and powerfully. Invariably, the status quo remains firmly entrenched when the STAKE isn't stated powerfully.

People love to talk about radical changes in their lifestyles and how they're going to achieve those changes. They might say they'll give up cigarettes and climb a mountain, for example. Usually, you'll find them still talking and smoking the next day. We humans don't change very easily. For the STAKE to be powerful enough to shatter the status quo, we have to believe that to remain in our current state is more dangerous than to embark on a risky journey that leads to an unknown future. As powerful as it may be, vision alone isn't enough.

Change has a considerable psychological impact on the human mind. To the fearful it is threatening because it means things may get worse. To the hopeful it is encouraging because things may get better. To the confident it is inspiring because the challenge exists to make things better.

                        ℘   King Whitney, Jr.

After you've enlisted others in your transformation effort, questions and doubts arise—all perfectly reasonable—among the same people who heeded your call and pledged their support. Even before they reach their offices, they recoil from the implications of their newly made agreement. They wonder, "Who will I be when we arrive?" They ask, "What role will I play?" They contemplate everything—from what they'll be asked to do to where their desks will be.

Before any change or transformation can occur, people must be convinced. The STAKE must therefore operate on organizational, community, and personal levels. Toward those ends, we closely examine our powerful STAKE conversation to dissect the patterns it reveals. From those revelations we make the case for change.

The Stake is sometimes described as the burning platform.

A man once jumped from the top of a burning oil platform in the middle of the night into the icy North Atlantic Ocean. When he was interviewed, he said his choice was simple: "I looked at the fire racing toward me and thought, 'certain death.' I looked over the rail at the debris-filled, icy water and thought, 'probable death.' So I jumped."

The STAKE illustration shows three basic ways that people listen:

- Analytical people listen with their brains.

- Emotional people listen with their hearts.

- Financially motivated people listen with their wallets.

When you're up to something big that requires the enrollment of a large group, there will be a mix of all three types of people. You must address each of their unique ways of listening.

Conversations about the STAKE lead most people to move quickly to avoid or *push* away from pain: "If we don't change, something bad is going to happen to us!" People will also *pull* toward experiences of pleasure: "If we realize our vision, look at all the good we can do," or, "Look at all the money we can make!" Powerful STAKE conversations must have negative aspects (what to avoid or *push* away from) and positive aspects (what people desire and want to *pull* toward them).

STAKE reveals six components of a robust answer to the question, "What's at STAKE?" When you make the case for your vision, you must speak to the Head, Heart, and Wallet, and address the negative aspects of staying put as well as the benefits of moving ahead.

During the financial meltdown in the first decade of the new millennium, local food banks knew that demand for their services was escalating beyond their capacity (*push*–Head); more and more people were going hungry as a result (*push*–Heart); donations were down (*push*–Wallet). At the same time, they envisioned new partnerships with restaurants and grocery stores, to eliminate waste by making better food available in greater quantities (*pull*–Head). They further imagined a transformation of their organizational purpose—from one of food distribution for sustenance to one of wellness nutrition services (*pull*–Heart)—all conducted in a cost-effective fashion (*pull*–Wallet).

Remember this: everyone will come to planning meetings and complain about the status quo. They'll engage in deep conversation about solving problems and causing transformational outcomes. They'll wave the flag and sing the rally song; however, unless, a powerfully rational, heartfelt, and financially compelling case for change is made, they'll go back to what they know and continue to complain about how things should be different.

Take care to consider all six aspects illustrated in the STAKE PRIME: Head, Heart, and Wallet and their corresponding push—pulls. Your chances of persuading people to embrace the vision and free themselves from the grip of the status quo will improve dramatically as you make the case for transformation.

The STAKE works at organizational and individual levels. Heed this warning: embark on the journey only when each critical member of the team has a clear understanding of what's at STAKE for them personally.

There are three conversions a person needs to experience:
the conversion of the head; the conversion of the heart;
and the conversion of the pocketbook.

                                         Martin Luther

DECLARATION

DECLARATION

Great leaders declare what will be and by when.
What declarations motivate you right now?

One of the most profound privileges I've experienced is witnessing a group's DECLARATION to achieve a clear outcome by a specific date. In the moment of DECLARATION, the order in which things are said and done is important. President Kennedy's DECLARATION was an American to the Moon and back by the end of the decade. Mahatma Gandhi's was a free India before his death. Babe Ruth's was the next pitch over the left-field wall. These leaders pointed; then they hit. Too many others swing often and, when they do hit one over the wall, they stand at home plate and point. That approach is *not* declarative leadership. The order matters.

When a DECLARATION is made with INTEGRITY, the language itself shifts from passive to powerful:

Passive Voice	-> **Powerful Voice**
Plan	-> **Declare**
Try	-> **Do**
I should	-> **I shall**
I'm going to	-> **I am**
We ought to	-> **We are**

But / If	-> **Regardless**
I support the effort	-> **I commit to the outcome**
With conditions	-> **Unconditionally**
Soon	-> **Now**

Through the prism of the PRIMES, let's look at the power of DECLARATION to get you where you want to be. You've responded to the inner call of wanderlust. With the help of the CORE PRIME, you've enrolled a team to co-create the future. With INTEGRITY, your intent is now your DECLARATION. You aspire, not to try, but to be and to do.

> *There you go man, keep as cool as you can.*
> *Face piles of trials with smiles.*
> *It riles them to believe that you perceive*
> *the web they weave*
> *And keep on thinking free.*

> ๑   The Moody Blues, "In The Beginning"
> *from the album On the Threshold of a Dream*

The PRIMES revealed in Chapter 2 outfitted you to inspire others to commit to your vision. The world doesn't know it yet, but it has already transformed, because you have declared date-certain outcomes.

- **THE CORE PRIME** shows us the five critical understandings a team must share.

- **PARITY** instructs us to maintain our balance and sense of proportion as we forge the agreements of the CORE PRIME.

- **FACTS, STORIES, AND BELIEFS** illuminate how people come to conclusions, and they expose the root cause of disagreement. This PRIME instructs us on how to work with people to resolve disagreements.

- **STAKE** is a blueprint for how to motivate people to break free of the comfort and constraints of current conditions and leap into the future.

- **DECLARATION** gives substance to the vision to which we've committed. It propels us toward a specific outcome by a certain date.

The five PRIMES above give us the ability to build our team and excite, focus, and commit everyone to do what it takes to achieve our clear vision for the future.

Now, it's time to move out.

Adventure is a path. Real adventure—self-determined, self-motivated, often risky—forces you to have firsthand encounters with the world. The world the way it is, not the way you imagine it. Your body will collide with the earth and you will bear witness. In this way you will be compelled to grapple with the limitless kindness and bottomless cruelty of humankind—and perhaps realize that you yourself are capable of both. This will change you. Nothing will ever again be black-and-white.

           ✎ MARK JENKINS

PART 2
OUTWARD BOUND

You've made your DECLARATION. You've enrolled a team. Now you move out. Perhaps you're surprised that you're actually embarked on your quest to dent the Universe. Second thoughts may creep into your mind. Dismiss them quickly. You're accountable to those whom you've enrolled, to live in INTEGRITY, and uphold your DECLARATION. You've decided to live large and powerfully. You've taken on a challenge, and your life will never be the same. You're now the cause of something important and significant.

> *What you've done becomes the judge of what you're going to do—especially in other people's minds. When you're traveling, you are what you are. People don't have your past to hold against you. No yesterdays on the road.*
> ✏ William Least Heat-Moon

You're at the trailhead of your journey. Your energy is high, but you're smart enough to know that your adventure will only exchange its treasures for your energy. You need to prepare for the time when energy must be allocated carefully and used efficiently. At some point along the path, stress will run high, conflict will arise, and time will be at a premium. You cannot avoid it. You can only expect it, prepare for it, and manage it.

Traveling is a brutality. It forces you to trust strangers and to lose sight of all that familiar comfort of home and friends. You are constantly off balance. Nothing is yours except the essential things—air, sleep, dreams, the sea, the sky—all things tending towards the eternal or what we imagine of it.

ℰ   Cesare Pavese

CHAPTER 3

OUTFITTING

Your team is strong, healthy, and well-equipped. You've read books on personal mastery, time management, and leadership. That's good. Still, obstacles are certain to appear along the path. Some will block the way and slow your progress. Knowing how to anticipate adversity is critical, along with the wisdom to know that, although hurdles can't be avoided, they can be surmounted. Because you know that challenges lie ahead, you and your team must agree on how you will behave when you encounter them.

Each member of the team will pack the personal gear they deem essential to fulfill the vision and to reach the To Be. No matter what else they pack, everyone must include five essential items:

1. Intentional **CULTURE**

2. Intolerance for **GOSSIP**

3. Working definition of **CONSENSUS**

4. Commitment to be a **LEADER** and not a **VICTIM**

5. Means to clean up any **BREACH** in INTEGRITY

Outfitting each member of the team with the PRIMES above ensures that energy is channeled in useful directions, and that each person on the team retains their power throughout the journey.

Behaviors
We Tolerate

Culture

Behaviors
We Do Not
Tolerate

CULTURE

CULTURE

When people gather, they draw an invisible line, which
separates what they will tolerate
from what they won't.
Where did your group draw the line today?

As a group travels along the way of any great adventure, the most powerful determinant of behavior is the line drawn by the team members themselves to separate what they'll tolerate from what they won't. This demarcation is termed CULTURE. There are dozens of books on CULTURE, but once I saw this PRIME sketched, its principles embedded themselves into my brain, and it has proven extremely useful.

Some groups are intentional, active, and explicit about their CULTURE. They rely on principles and values to guide decision making and action steps. Other groups are more passive and allow their CULTURE to evolve. The latter groups typically institute policies and codify rules into a formal system that requires inspection, verification, and enforcement by outside entities. The result is rarely as powerful as an intentional CULTURE.

For an intentional CULTURE to thrive, people must talk about what they'll tolerate and call out others when they cross the line. Group members must be willing to declare, "This is how we do things," or, "We don't do that!"

It's important to make CULTURE explicit from the beginning of any change or transformation initiative. The group needs to recognize that CULTURE is a living thing; it's shaped all the time, whether actively or passively, and everyone has a role in its development. Although CULTURE is made up of many elements, five characteristics are common among high-performance cultures:

1.   They don't tolerate **GOSSIP**.

2.   They know how to forge **CONSENSUS**.

3.   Members live in **INTEGRITY** with one another.

4.   They support each other as **LEADERS** and don't tolerate **VICTIM** attitudes.

5.   They quickly recognize and clean up any **BREACH** of INTEGRITY.

These attributes are discussed more fully in each of the four PRIMES that follow.

A culture is made—or destroyed—by its articulate voices.

                                                             Ayn Rand

GOSSIP

GOSSIP

Gossip thrives not in the "saying" but in the "listening."
Are you listening for what strengthens or diminishes others?

Jeff Conklin, a contemporary and partner of mine on many projects, literally wrote the book on the business of complex problem solving.[13] Jeff and I visited with his dad, Bob Conklin, in Ashland, Virginia, one afternoon, on our way home from an appointment south of Washington, D.C. That day, the GOSSIP PRIME was revealed to me.

Bob and his wife started an intentional community back in the 1960s, called Ashland Vineyards. Very few of the hundreds of communes begun in that era survived. Ashland Vineyards is still thriving, and I was curious to learn what Bob Conklin knew about establishing and sustaining an intentional CULTURE. At the time, I was wrestling with how to keep my own company's wonderful CULTURE alive and well while we navigated a steep growth curve.

After we talked about boat building and poetry, I asked Bob, "So, how have you kept this community alive all these years?"

He replied succinctly, "We tolerate no GOSSIP." Bob Conklin clearly placed enormous value on this simple and essential principle.

GOSSIP is pure, destructive energy. It destroys possibility, and its victims are left diminished in the eyes of the group. GOSSIP is the most destructive behavior any group can choose to tolerate.

Even though GOSSIP is such a damaging force, it's pervasive and tolerated to some degree in most organizations. Attempts to eliminate it often prove ineffective, because many people who engage in GOSSIP fail to recognize their own behavior and even those who do underestimate its negative effects. GOSSIP stops when no one listens. The keys to eliminate GOSSIP are to teach everyone how to recognize it and to secure their agreement not to participate in it. It's as simple as this: when anyone begins to complain about another person, no matter the reason, ask, "Before you go on, will either of us approach him directly about this?" If the answer is no, stop listening. Eliminating GOSSIP creates the possibility to sustain a CULTURE in which group members actively invest in the development of all other members.

When you're up to something big, a CULTURE of zero-tolerance for GOSSIP is critical.

Fire and swords are slow engines of destruction, compared to the tongue of a Gossip.

❧   Sir Richard Steele

1. ☑ The process was explicit, rational, and fair;

2. ☑ I was treated well and my inputs were heard;

3. ☑ I can live with and commit to the outcomes.

CONSENSUS

CONSENSUS

Everyone in agreement on everything is so overrated.
Can you and your team disagree but "live with" the process
and the outcome?

The most challenging environments in which to pursue transformation and problem solving are institutes of higher learning and multilateral organizations like the World Bank, the International Finance Corporation, and the United Nations. They're stuffed full with brilliant people. Yet, as Peter Keen, a gifted colleague at the World Bank, once remarked, "Intelligence is like having four-wheel drive: you usually end up stuck like everybody else, just in a more remote location."

When I sat with Michael Doyle one frustrating afternoon, and lamented my inability to secure a critical decision at the World Bank, he asked gently, "What are you trying to do?"

I replied, "I'm just trying to get everyone to agree!"

Michael looked at me penetratingly and said, "Why would you ever try to do that?" Then he took a napkin and drew the sketch illustrated on the previous page. He called it a working definition of CONSENSUS. He helped me see the group's lack of agreement in a new way. I immediately understood that my job was to make sure that everyone agreed with three points regarding any decision:

1. **Process Satisfaction:** each stakeholder believes that the decision-making process is explicit, rational, and fair.

2. **Personal Treatment:** each stakeholder feels treated honorably, meaning they have ample opportunity to be heard, to make their opinions known, and to consider the opinions of others.

3. **Outcome Satisfaction:** each participant can live with the outcome. Notice the words, *live with,* as opposed to *agree with.*

Michael's point was that, if people are satisfied with the first two elements above, they typically agree to the third.

The "dark side" of this PRIME is also important to watch for: people may say they can live with the outcome, but if they remain significantly dissatisfied, even privately, with either of the first two elements, the dissatisfaction will undermine their commitment and detract from their participation. The result is neither desirable nor affordable when team members must work well together to produce extraordinary outcomes.

Today, we outfit all of our consultants with the CONSENSUS PRIME, and I never leave home without it.

I can't give you a surefire formula for success, but I can give you a formula for failure: try to please everybody all the time.

                          ❧   Herbert Bayard Swope

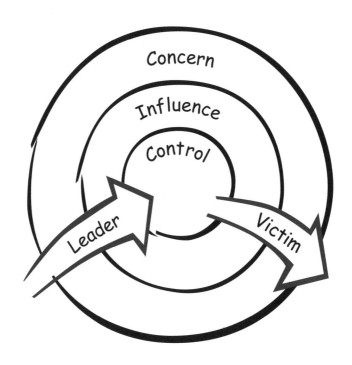

VICTIM - LEADER

VICTIM–LEADER

*Conversations move either toward a tone of
helplessness or empowerment. Listen closely.
Do your team members sound like victims or leaders?*

Great leaders and high-performance teams listen carefully to the tone and direction of their conversations. They can identify when a group begins to lose its power by complaining about things it can't affect, and blaming others for its own lack of effectiveness. This is the sound of a VICTIM: "If Congress would just do their job, we could do ours." There's nothing to be gained by wishing that things we can't control were different.

Good leaders identify when groups operate from a sense of empowerment and a can-do attitude; great leaders help victim-oriented groups regain their power and help empowered groups sustain theirs. The VICTIM–LEADER PRIME is the "nuclear PRIME" because, when it's brought to a group's attention, they hate it. They absolutely hate it! It's much easier to be a VICTIM than to be a LEADER.

In any conversation, groups move toward being LEADERS or VICTIMS. They talk either about things they can do, or about what's being done to them. Once this PRIME is distinguished, the group becomes directly responsible for tolerating victimhood. This awareness makes what once was easy become suddenly unpleasant and intolerable.

To take responsibility at all times—to be the cause—may feel like a huge burden. VICTIM–LEADER therefore is one of the few PRIMES best introduced in explicit fashion sparingly. This PRIME is valuable even when you keep it to yourself. So even if you don't speak of it, pay close attention to which way the group is headed. Guide them to talk about things they can control. That's where their power is stored.

You are not a victim of the world; you lead it. You are not imagining the future; you are causing it.

                                             ❧   Chris McGoff

BREACH

BREACH

People are not always their word.
How resilient are you and your team?

BREACH is a failure to do what you said you'd do. If you're late to a meeting, for example, after you committed to be on time, your tardiness is perceived as a BREACH of INTEGRITY. If you say, "I quit smoking," and later you're seen smoking, the conflict is remembered as a BREACH between your declaration and your action. Just as INTEGRITY builds trust, BREACH erodes it. BREACH makes you undependable and diminishes you in the eyes of the group. You lose power, and teams can't afford to have members, much less leaders, with diminished power.

The BREACH PRIME is noticed only against the backdrop of INTEGRITY. If you're *always* late for meetings, no one really notices or cares; that's just what you do and who you are. You're Mr. or Ms. Late. If you say you're *trying* to quit smoking, and people see you smoking, they don't consider your behavior a BREACH, because *trying* to quit is a powerless idea.

To point out your own BREACH is to treat your word seriously. When others point out your BREACH, they're enrolled in and committed to a CULTURE of INTEGRITY.

Despite a commitment and a willingness to maintain INTEGRITY, it's probable and perhaps even inevitable that a BREACH will occur. Cleaning up after a BREACH quickly, reestablishing INTEGRITY, and restoring an individual's place in the group are steps taken in everyone's best interest. It isn't the BREACH of integrity that a high-performance culture doesn't tolerate but failing to acknowledge it and reestablish INTEGRITY.

ACKNOWLEDGE AND RECOMMIT

1. Acknowledge a BREACH:

> *"I said I'd be here at nine o'clock, and I wasn't."*

Acknowledging a BREACH is the first step toward repair. When people fail to acknowledge their BREACH, group members may do it for them. Acknowledgment creates a clearing for an individual to reestablish his or her INTEGRITY and thus regain his or her power in the group. A timely stand for someone's INTEGRITY is one of the highest acts of love and concern that group members can give each other.

2. Recommit to INTEGRITY

> *"In the future, I'll be on time."*

That's it. No excuses. Excuses deflect accountability and waste more of the group's time.

If someone feels the need to apologize, it can be done between the first and second step. It's unnecessary most of the time, however, since an apology is implied in acknowledging a BREACH.

> *A single lie destroys a whole reputation of integrity.*
>   ✎   Baltasar Gracian

The five PRIMES in this chapter prepare you to recognize and manage inevitable obstacles on whatever path you take.

· **CULTURE** outfits us with our responsibility to be explicit about the behavior we will and will not tolerate; to be intentional about the CULTURE we're generating.

· **GOSSIP** is a destructive force we recognize and refuse.

· **CONSENSUS** is an explicit and rational process for discussing options when a group faces important choices. Team members treat each other fairly and are committed to the outcome, even if they don't agree with everything.

· **VICTIM-LEADER** calls for a team's commitment to be the cause of what's happening and what's going to happen. Team members waste no time complaining about things they can't control or influence.

· **BREACH** makes INTEGRITY a cornerstone of the group's CULTURE. The group is committed to maintain its members' power. If and when a BREACH occurs, everyone knows how to acknowledge and repair it quickly.

Creating a new theory is not like destroying an old barn and erecting a skyscraper in its place. It is rather like climbing a mountain, gaining new and wider views, discovering unexpected connections between our starting points and its rich environment. But the point from which we started out still exists and can be seen, although it appears smaller and forms a tiny part of our broad view gained by the mastery of the obstacles on our adventurous way up.

∾   Albert Einstein

CHAPTER 4

STEPPING OFF

You've answered the call, made a DECLARATION, and enrolled others to help achieve it. You're outfitted and prepared to step off. Stepping off requires you to face great challenges. You recognize that the trek will be long and difficult, and you take the first step anyway.

The challenges that you and your team will face are intellectual and physical. It's essential to focus all available energy on realizing the DECLARATION. In this chapter, we reveal PRIMES that will help concentrate the team's energy on the most important activities.

> *Do not follow where the path may lead; go instead where there is no path and leave a trail.*
> **❧ RALPH WALDO EMERSON**

MUDA

MUDA
無駄
(Japanese for nonvalue-added activity)

Nonvalue-added activity keeps creeping into your group. What will you stop doing—and what will you make room for—that adds value today?

The status quo is loaded with people who spend time and money on nonvalue-added activities. The Japanese call this "MUDA": resources allocated to things that do not address the needs of the mission or the team. MUDA is like "corporate cholesterol." It builds up slowly, silently, and continuously until it chokes the system and contributes to a cloying sense of powerlessness.

The activities involved in problem solving, change, and transformation require tremendous energy. All systems have finite resources. When we're up to something big, we have to let go of things that no longer serve us in order to create space for things that do. The situations we face may be described as follows:

- Like a selfish child, the As Is threatens to require all available resources and then some.

- At the same time, pressure grows for us to conserve resources.

- Developments occur in our environment that make our own change and transformation imperative, but these efforts require even more resources.

These conditions create the kind of "perfect storm" that businesses and organizations face every day. It may become a matter of survival to free up scarce resources quickly, to invest in problem solving, and effect change and transformation, even as we protect a mission and a team from added risk.

Fellow Universe Denter Kai Dosier was the first to help me recognize MUDA. Kai has a habit of being around substantial change and transformation efforts at large companies and brings an intense customer focus to the organizations he serves. The MUDA PRIME illuminates a way to quickly and continually ensure that all available resources are concentrated on the most important aspects of business and customer needs.

We must first recognize that the status quo wants us to think that no resources are available for doing anything other than keeping things like they are. That thinking serves only to maintain the As Is. Once we recognize that the status quo is lying to us, MUDA isn't that hard to eliminate:

- First, list all business needs and requirements.

- Second, list all customer needs.

- Next, list all the things you actually do.

- Then look at the overlap between the lists.

- Finally, take action:

  1. STOP spending time and money on nonvalue-added activities.

  2. START investing freed-up time and money on unfulfilled business and customer needs.

We cannot wait for the world to turn, for times to change that we might change with them, for the revolution to come and carry us around to its new course. We ourselves are the future.

                                  Beatrice Bruteau

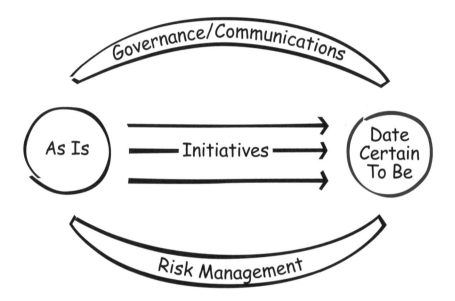

REDPOINT

REDPOINT

The question is not,
"What is important to do?"
The question is,
"Of all that is important,
what are the fewest most important
things to do now?"
Are you doing a few things about everything,
or everything about a few things?

In the mid 1970s, German rock climbing legend Kurt Albert painted red marks at the base of routes he became skilled enough to climb without using any supports or aids, other than his hands, feet, and body. In many ways, Albert's REDPOINT system was the origin of the free-climbing movement that led to the development of sport climbing a decade later. For our purposes, REDPOINT refers to a path marked for leaders and teams to overcome challenges, attain their visions, and dent the Universe.

The REDPOINT PRIME can be summed up in one word: "focus." It reveals the fastest, least risky path from our As Is to our To Be.

Recall that the CORE PRIME makes the need clear to go from the As Is to the To Be, because something important is at Stake. Creative tension exists in a call to action. The Strategy arrow represents actions that will liberate a

team from the As Is and enable it to realize the possibilities of the To Be.
REDPOINT reveals how to make that journey.

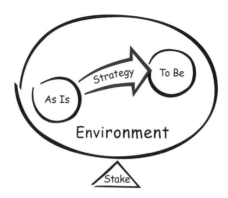

Before we examine the insights of the REDPOINT PRIME, it's important
to understand how dangerous the journey can be from the As Is to the To
Be. Let's look at some examples of the challenges we face:

> Since the 1980s, it's been clear to all involved that the Air
> Traffic Control System in the United States is in need of
> complete overhaul. It's outdated, dangerous, and will force
> customers to pay more to fly. The STAKE seems clear:
> airplanes are sometimes guided by computers made before
> cell phones, which people replace every 18 months or less. In
> the 1990s, the United States spent $2.9 billion to overhaul
> the system but pulled the plug on a failed attempt.

> The Government Accountability Office reported in 2009 that
> the Federal Bureau of Investigation abandoned its "Virtual
> Case File" system after spending four years and $170 million
> to make it work. At the same time, the Department of

Veterans Affairs abandoned its efforts to implement a patient appointment schedule system, after spending eight years and $167 million.

There are dozens more examples like those above, and the carnage isn't restricted to government. The numbers from private industry are just as shocking. Various sources document an approximate failure rate of 70 percent for information technology (IT) projects. One study found that as many as 50 percent of all IT projects are considered "runaways," meaning they fit any two of the following descriptions:

- More than 180 percent of the targeted time was required to complete a project.

- More than 160 percent of the estimated budget was consumed.

- Less than 70 percent of the targeted functionality was delivered.[14]

The carnage is also not limited to technology. Statistics show a failure rate of between 40 and 80 percent for most mergers and acquisitions. When defined in terms of shareholder value, the failure rate is 83 percent.[15]

Love of bustle is not industry.

 ❧   Seneca

The PRIMES you're outfitted with thus far will enable you to avoid many of the mistakes that result in disasters like those cited above. The challenge is formidable; the road is dangerous.

Got it. Let's press on.

The REDPOINT PRIME is made up of six elements, two of which are also found in the CORE PRIME: As Is and To Be. Let's examine the other four elements.

INITIATIVES

Initiatives are projects with objectives, start times, milestones, and specific finish times. Assigning the most effective Initiatives to a REDPOINT requires us to ask penetrating questions. Rather than ask, for example, "What are the important things we need to do to reach our goal?" seasoned Universe Denters ask, "Of all the important things we need to do to break out of the As Is and propel us unstoppably toward our To Be, what are the fewest, most important things (one to three) we must accomplish in the next 6, 12, or 18 months?"

The latter question forces ruthless prioritization. Pay careful attention to time frames.

Regardless of how long we must work to achieve our To Be, it's critical to set interim REDPOINTS that can be achieved in six months, and they should never exceed 18 months; more than that and focus is lost. Each REDPOINT should be designed so that its accomplishment is a cause for celebration.

Initiatives should have leaders, called "Lane Drivers." In large projects, "Portfolio Managers" may be assigned as resources for Lane Drivers, and to coordinate their interaction and interdependence.

In the REDPOINT illustration, Initiatives are wrapped within a framework of three more elements: Governance, Communications, and Risk Management.

GOVERNANCE

Those with the most power, resources, and the most to lose must be ready to use overwhelming influence to resolve problems quickly, which people in the "lanes" may not be able or equipped to handle.

COMMUNICATIONS

Those responsible for developing and sharing the narrative, or story, about what's going on, do so in a manner that maintains maximum commitment, power, and momentum, while eliminating resistance.

RISK MANAGEMENT

Those who look forward anticipate risks and intervene proactively to mitigate threats to schedules, quality, and costs.

At its core, REDPOINT embodies a simple concept: rather than do a few things about everything, the most powerful leaders and teams do everything about the fewest, most important things. They willingly live with complete INTEGRITY to realize their declared To Be on time.

REDPOINT is unique, in six distinct ways, from principles typically used to implement most strategic initiatives:

1.   Who Helps Whom?

Leadership teams usually delegate the implementation of strategic initiatives. Leaders often feel it's enough to see status reports and to "be available" to help implementation teams, should the need arise. This approach rarely works. REDPOINT implementation teams hold themselves directly accountable for success, while everyone else helps them, including their leaders. Vigilance is required to maintain this orientation.

The REDPOINT PRIME is virtually guaranteed to work when leaders, with authority and commitment to date-certain outcomes, take proactive measures to clear roadblocks from the path of transformation initiatives.

2.   Overwhelming Power

In typical problem solving and change efforts, governance teams, when they exist at all, meet at regular intervals and spend most of their time in an attempt to arrive at a common starting point. REDPOINT governance teams convene only when problems arise, and their success is measured by how quickly they resolve them.

3.   Information as Oil

Outside of REDPOINT, those responsible for communications are rarely held accountable for the amount of resistance to strategic initiatives, or for establishing power through information sharing. Effective communication smoothes the path for everyone, and encourages understanding and acceptance of the changes that happen around them.

4.   Orientation

"Scorekeepers" usually look backward and report on what has happened. REDPOINT scorekeepers look forward, anticipating what's ahead and finding ways to mitigate risk.

5.   Lock-On Date

Deadlines don't budge in a project that recognizes the REDPOINT PRIME. In other environments, when someone comes up with a new and valuable idea, the team extends the project deadline to accommodate it. When a new idea comes into a REDPOINT-based project, the first question is, "Can we do it and keep to our schedule?" If not, the idea is recorded for later use. When a deadline is in jeopardy, REDPOINT demands a decrease in scope that doesn't jeopardize the value of the outcome. People become amazingly innovative when a leader takes this position.

Lock-On Date is the "incubator of innovation."

6.   The End is Near

In a well-run, REDPOINT-based project, a sense of urgency helps teams to maintain a fast operation tempo right from the start. When a natural lull occurs, every six months or so, it's a time to acknowledge the team's efforts and make adjustments on the basis of what lies ahead.

For some leaders, the REDPOINT PRIME may provide the "shock of recognition" mentioned in the Prologue, "...when a PRIME jumps off the page, confirming what you have long felt was true but could never quite articulate." Perhaps you've worked on projects that didn't adhere to these principles and you know how that felt.

The REDPOINT PRIME tends to grow on you. The next time you're asked to join or lead a team, take another look at REDPOINT. If you're part of a team now, compare and contrast how yours is organized; imagine how it might function if REDPOINT principles were introduced.

The next several PRIMES will reveal more deeply the insights contained in REDPOINT.

I can't change the direction of the wind, but I can adjust my sails to always reach my destination.

ဆ   Jimmy Dean

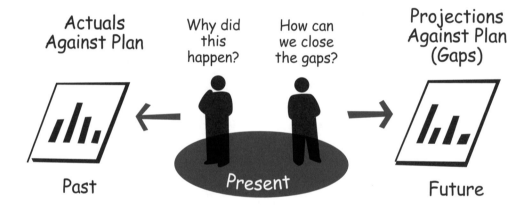

ISSUES FORWARD

ISSUES FORWARD

Looking behind and ahead are both important.
Where do you and your group
spend your time and energy?

Bob Kelly, a senior executive at Arthur Anderson, hosted a gourmet dinner one night in a private dining room of the Jefferson Hotel in Washington, D.C. Around the table was a collection of high-powered, Type A business leaders, engaged in a spirited debate about an important and pressing issue. Discussion became intense. Ever the gracious host, Bob listened quietly while he made sure that our servings were ample and our wine glasses were replenished. As the dessert course arrived amid arguments around the table, Bob raised his hand slowly and said, "ISSUES FORWARD." The room went quiet. With that simple phrase, we redirected our focus to what we could affect and what we needed to do.

Years later, Peter DiGiammarino, then a member of my firm's board of directors, had a similar effect on a conversation and on the way I managed my business. A great teacher and a patient man, Peter helped me understand that leaders either look at performance reports from the past or projections for the future. Most leaders spend their time on performance reports, perhaps because a backward glance is attractive; information is available and confirmed. Projections against plan are speculative, but they're much more valuable.

There are two questions for leaders to ask about the performance of their organizations or systems:

1. *Why did things go this way, compared with the plan?*
This question comes after review of a performance report to evaluate what happened. As a form of reflective learning, it's a valuable question and should be asked.

ISSUES FORWARD can be even more valuable:

2. *What's projected; what's the plan now, and how do we close the gap?*
This question is powerful and proactive.

Leaders with an ISSUES FORWARD outlook ask in November for December's revenue target and the current projection. Then—and this is the key—effective leaders immediately call for action to close the gap between the plan and projection when a potential shortfall is spotted. They ask their managers, "What do we have to do now to eliminate the gap between our projection and our plan?" This question illustrates the principle of the ISSUES FORWARD PRIME and leaders who ask it are rarely surprised.

Powerful leaders tend to have four words clearly defined:

1. **Plan:** What we intend to make happen in the future;

2. **Projection:** What we think is really going to happen unless we do something different;

3. **Actuality:** What really happened when we look backward and assess; and

4. **Reforecast:** What we do when projections are so far off from plan; a new number must be declared to reestablish healthy tension in the system, but we never forget the original plan.

Leaders may compare actual performance to plan, see the gap, and ask, "Why?" Or they can compare projections to the plan, see the gap, and ask, "How do we close the gap?"

ISSUES FORWARD leads to immediate, decisive action.

> *The more you are willing to accept responsibility for your actions, the more credibility you will have.*
> ᔐ   Brian Koslow

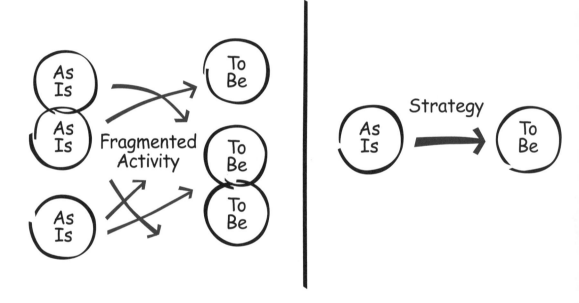

COHESION

COHESION

*Our chances of getting what we want increase when we agree
on what we want and work together to achieve it.
Cohesion is unnatural for groups. How good are you at
establishing and sustaining it?*

COHESION may be one of the most critical elements to manage, as a group charges against its challenges. COHESION is present when everyone gives the same answers to the following three questions:

1.   Where are we starting from?

2.   Where are we going?

3.   What do we have to do to get there?

COHESION among group members is an unnatural phenomenon that requires constant energy to maintain. Without their investment in COHESION, individuals tend to have slightly—or significantly—different views of their current situation and of the urgency to change. They also have different views of what they're creating. This behavior is natural, but when these differences prevail, they fragment the group's focus, dissipate its energy, and create an environment ripe for conflict. The COHESION PRIME reminds us that people work on different activities for different reasons and at different intensities. Expect FRAGMENTATION but drive for

COHESION and do whatever it takes, as many times as it takes, to establish it.

In this chapter, we revealed four PRIMES to help fuel the group, and to focus and maintain its energy, as it attempts the extraordinary.

- **MUDA** showed us how to recognize and eliminate nonvalue-added activity.

- **REDPOINT** revealed the importance of doing everything about the fewest, most important things rather than a few things about everything. With REDPOINT as the guide, how you organize may determine the survival of your effort.

- **ISSUES FORWARD** enables us to ask, "What must we do now to make sure we'll be where we need to be later?"

- **COHESION** emphasizes the values of unity of purpose and alignment. It goes against nature's tendency toward FRAGMENTATION; therefore, COHESION requires time and energy to establish and maintain.

We're well on our way toward our declared To Be. Typically, things get tricky when we near our destination. We need to watch for danger signs as we approach a phase when projects can completely unravel.

And it ought to be remembered that there is nothing more difficult to take in hand, more perilous to conduct, or more uncertain in its success, than to take the lead in the introduction of a new order of things. Because the innovator has for enemies all those who have done well under the old conditions, and lukewarm defenders in those who may do well under the new. This coolness arises partly from fear of the opponents, who have the laws on their side, and partly from the incredulity of men, who do not readily believe in new things until they have had a long experience of them.

℘ Niccolo Machiavelli

CHAPTER 5

HERE BE DRAGONS

One of the greatest benefits of thorough preparation is readiness to encounter and manage the inevitable "dragons"[16]—people who conceal their agenda until the worst possible moment, often without realizing that this is what they're doing. Dragons threaten every effort to dent the Universe; they're independent thinkers who appear within even the most cohesive group.

Dragons will manifest most often when you and your team are tired, hungry, and at your weakest. You can't *eliminate* them, but you'll be able to *anticipate* them, and you'll have the PRIMES to *manage* them. When you put the next five PRIMES in your back pocket, you'll be thoroughly prepared to deal with the dragons. Mastering these PRIMES will enable you to turn arguments into dialogues, dialogues into shared understanding, and shared understanding into shared vision and agreements; all of which becomes synchronized and coordinated action.

... the secret that has puzzled all the philosophers, baffled all the lawyers, muddled all the men of business, and ruined most of the artists: the secret of right and wrong.

                              George Bernard Shaw

BIG HAT - LITTLE HAT

BIG HAT–LITTLE HAT

Whether they know it or not,
your team members can wear two hats.
Who's wearing which hat right now?

BIG HAT–LITTLE HAT represents a powerful right-versus-right dilemma that groups confront constantly. It's fun to put on a BIG HAT, think like the CEO, and make decisions that are good for the company. It's natural and unavoidable, however, to put on a LITTLE HAT and assess corporate actions as to how they affect us and our team. People wearing different hats will never see the same issue the same way. Until both viewpoints are named, the conflict between them is pervasive yet relatively invisible.

> *It isn't that they can't see the solution. It's that they can't*
> *see the problem.*
>
>   ✎   G. K. Chesterton

BIG HAT–LITTLE HAT once plagued a transformation initiative at the U.S. Army National Guard:

General William Navas was a passionate leader, with a deep understanding of the U.S. Constitution and the framers' intent. When General Navas directed the Guard, it was made up of 360,000 soldiers under the leadership of 54 adjutant generals (TAGS). Most of the time, the TAGS reported to the state governors. This was Thomas Jefferson's way to ensure that the President couldn't send troops in against the states. In time of war, however, the Guard could be mobilized under federal control. Since its inception, the National Guard has functioned with this embedded split: On one hand, it's a collection of 52 armies, free to make independent decisions in their state's best interests. On the other hand, the Guard is a military force that must snap into alignment with the U.S. Army. General Navas was responsible for making it all work.

The TAGS wore SMALL HATS when they made choices in the best interests of their particular states. They wore BIG HATS when they joined General Navas in his effort to modernize and transform the entire system within the confines of severely constrained budgets. Our team provided the consultants to support General Navas' initiative. The STAKES were high. What concerned General Navas most was that, if he couldn't build cohesive intent and focus within the TAG community, negotiations with the Pentagon regarding budget would become more difficult than they were already.

Under General Navas' direction, we employed the principle,

"What you resist persists." We embraced the BIG HAT–LITTLE HAT dilemma. We made a huge sketch of the PRIME and hung it on the wall in the planning room; then we dissected its component parts.

Once the elements of BIG HAT–LITTLE HAT were delineated, we asked the group to self-regulate and give out yellow and red cards for inappropriate LITTLE HAT behavior. Oh, we had fun with that! Quickly, new values emerged: the group began to move away from exclusive, "either/or" solutions, and to search for inclusive, "both/and" solutions.

I don't think the National Guard transformation initiative would've succeeded without embracing the BIG HAT–LITTLE HAT PRIME. The TAGS came together and figured it out. Their solidarity was evident in the plans and budgets they built and in the negotiations they had with the Department of Defense. These same plans and budgets are now considered an integral part of America's Army, while National Guard troops maintain their vital role as state-based first responders, at the service of the governors.

One of Michael Doyle's insights, BIG HAT–LITTLE HAT contains four elements:

1. It's a right-versus-right dilemma, as opposed to right-versus-wrong.

2. The implicit dichotomy of this PRIME can't be eliminated, only managed.

3. People need to be clear about which hat they're wearing when they speak.

4. It's fair to advocate for your LITTLE HAT but not to the detriment of the whole.

Leaders must become adept at wearing BIG HATS and LITTLE HATS to manage teams effectively through Right vs. Right challenges. Despite the National Guard success story, BIG HAT–LITTLE HAT remains one of the top four challenges that appear along the path to transformative outcomes. The next PRIME reveals the rest.

*Don't tell people how to do things, tell them what to do
and let them surprise you with their results.*

ℰ   George S. Patton

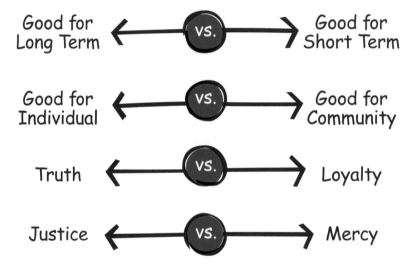

RIGHT VS. RIGHT

RIGHT VS. RIGHT

"RIGHT VS. RIGHT" dilemmas,
managed as "right vs. wrong" arguments,
tear a group apart.
How skilled are you at handling inevitable collisions of values?

When conversations deteriorate into disagreements that disintegrate into arguments, the great misperception is that one position must be right and others must be wrong. While right-versus-wrong issues certainly create opportunities for disagreement, mistaking a RIGHT VS. RIGHT dilemma for a right-versus-wrong issue can be as debilitating and destructive as GOSSIP. Quick recognition that a collision of two "rights" is the source of an escalating argument enables a leader to intervene, resolve the tension, and reorient the team toward its To Be.

The power of right-versus-right dilemmas was first revealed to me by Rushworth Kidder, of the Institute for Global Ethics in Rockland, Maine.[17] I sought out Dr. Kidder in response to a request by one of our senior military clients. The client noticed an increasing incidence of inappropriate and, at times, illegal and immoral behavior among some personnel. He wanted an external review of his organization's stated values as a way to begin to address the worrisome trends.

Dr. Kidder pointed out that an organization's values are rarely the source of ethical problems. His research showed that, throughout the world, core values are almost universal. For example, "truth" and "loyalty" are highly prized across almost all societies. Serious problems arise, however, when these values—these "rights"—collide. Here's a perfect example of colliding rights:

> How are military personnel instructed to behave, for example, when a commanding officer orders a subordinate to lie? The subordinate faces an intractable dilemma between loyalty to an officer and loyalty to the truth.

Before I knew him, Dr. Kidder began to investigate just how clearly the military set out resolution principles to handle ethical dilemmas like the one illustrated above. His research helped set the U.S. military on a clear path to bolster its culture.

What happens when the needs of the team conflict with the needs of a specific individual? RIGHT VS. RIGHT dilemmas can show up anywhere; the issues confront us throughout our experience.

> Consider little Susie, whose parents teach her to be a good friend and always tell the truth. What happens when Susie's third grade teacher asks her if her best friend, Tommy, just copied the answers from her test? Susie knows he did. Does loyalty to Tommy trump telling the truth or vice versa?

In his book, *How Good People Make Tough Choices*, Rush Kidder makes clear the ethical dilemmas we face every day. The first step in managing these challenges is to recognize them when they occur. By naming these RIGHT VS. RIGHT dilemmas, we make them visible and recognizable.

No single answer exists to resolve RIGHT VS. RIGHT dilemmas. The next PRIME, however, for which Rush Kidder deserves all the credit, shows how to handle and resolve colliding rights. Resolution is critical, because getting stuck and standing still for too long is dangerous and may be fatal to your efforts.

> *Life is a constant oscillation between the sharp horns of dilemmas.*
>
> ✌ H. L. Mencken

Ends-Based:
Do the
greatest
good for the
most people.

Rule-Based:
Act as if
creating
a universal
standard.

Care-Based:
Do unto others
as you want
them to do
unto you.

RESOLUTION PRINCIPLES

RESOLUTION PRINCIPLES

*Leadership requires us to act boldly in the face of ethical dilemmas.
How effectively do you resolve those that threaten your group?*

Most likely, you'll encounter one or more dilemmas on the path to your declared outcome. The RESOLUTION PRINCIPLES PRIME can help you find the highest "right" when faced with the toughest choices.

As a leader, you may face the challenge of dealing with an underperforming employee. His or her underperformance may be due to factors outside the employee's control, such as the aftermath of a house fire. Such a situation puts a leader between colliding "rights": compassion for the employee, the business need for higher performance, and the needs of other employees who may be affected by someone's underperformance.

There are only three ways to make the best choice when faced with such a RIGHT VS. RIGHT dilemma:

End-based: Select the option that generates the most good for the most people.

Rule-based: Choose as if you're creating a universal standard.

Care-based: Choose as if you were the one most affected by your decision.

Intractable ethical dilemmas are unavoidable, but you'll recognize them and help others see them too. You'll make your team aware of RESOLUTION PRINCIPLES and help them apply the one that best fits any situation. It's an amazing gift to deliver.

And little wonder…that as we practice resolving dilemmas we find ethics to be less of a goal than a pathway, less of a destination than a trip, less an inoculation than a process.

　　　　　　　　　　　　　　　　ॐ　　Rushworth M. Kidder

BLIND MEN AND THE ELEPHANT

BLIND MEN
AND THE ELEPHANT

People usually agree when they have the same information. Can you get people to "not agree" without "dis-agreeing?"

The blind man holding the elephant's trunk has every reason to identify it as a snake. The same may be said for the blind man who stands next to the elephant's leg and perceives it to be a tree. The two men arrive at different conclusions because they have different information. Once members of a team observe this dynamic and recognize that they each hold only a *part* of the elephant, they often resolve their differences quickly.

The principle of this ancient fable is particularly visible in governments and large organizations; large systems made up of other, smaller systems. A few years ago, I witnessed the awesome power of BLIND MEN AND THE ELEPHANT.

> The top 70 leaders of the World Bank were gathered together, for the first time, to chart the institution's future. Each leader usually advocated for a particular region of the world or for a specific area of the issue of poverty. I remember the sense of being overwhelmed by the needs of those in developing nations.

We gathered in a large room and hung huge sheets of paper on the walls from ceiling to floor. A team of artists painted a real-time picture of the conversation, which followed the framework of the CORE PRIME. We discussed matters and explored possibilities for three days. At the conclusion, the north wall contained a collective description of the needs of the world and the Bank's entire As Is. The east wall captured the STAKE conversation. The south wall illustrated a deep, colorful rendering of the collective vision. The west wall displayed a shared strategy.

We sat together during the last hours of the meeting and took it all in. For the first time, the World Bank's top leaders could "see" the whole. I witnessed firsthand the profound effect of a massive, shared perspective. From that moment on, the CULTURE of the World Bank became more collaborative, as cooperation extended across traditional boundaries.

Rather than focus on how to help a group avoid disagreements, learn to focus on how to manage them and help facilitate a resolution. When people disagree, the first step is to determine what information they have to form their position. Before you attempt to forge a common agreement, work to ensure that everyone has access to the same information, the content of which they can agree to, at least generally. The effort may take time; however, once everyone has the same information, more often than not they tend to reach similar conclusions.

A person's perception is their reality.

         Michael Doyle

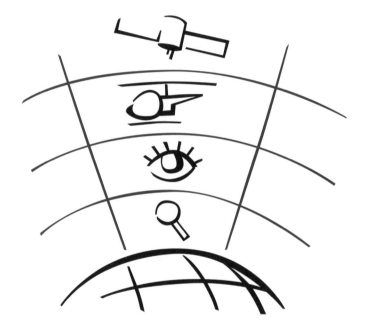

LEVELS OF PERSPECTIVE

LEVELS OF PERSPECTIVE

*We see different things from close up than from high above. What's the
best vantage point for you and your team right now?*

The LEVELS OF PERSPECTIVE PRIME is similar to BLIND MEN
AND THE ELEPHANT. There are two things to remember here:

1.   Arriving at the right perspective is important and takes thought.

2.   Bringing everyone to the same level of perspective enhances discussions
     and helps avoid arguments.

Consider this example:

> You're stuck in traffic at an intersection. Late for a meeting,
> frustrated and impatient, you look around in vain for a police
> officer to take control of the situation and get everyone moving.
> When you tune the radio to the traffic channel, you learn that
> the cause of the backup is an accident miles ahead. Even if an
> officer were to arrive at your intersection, there would be little
> that he or she could do.

It's usually best to begin with an overall perspective, like the one to be had
from the satellite or helicopter in the illustration on the previous page. When

points of leverage (the car radio in the example above) and the root cause of a problem (the news of an accident miles ahead) become apparent, zoom in and address them (like the eye and the magnifying glass in the illustration). Too often, I see people use detailed management tools indiscriminately, such as Six Sigma and Total Quality Management. While these programs can be extremely helpful, they are frequently implemented without determining where they will provide the greatest positive effect. As a result, too often they're simply used to shift problems from one management group to another.

The PRIMES revealed in this chapter clarify the importance of focusing and expending energy efficiently. We discovered the dragons: RIGHT VS. RIGHT dilemmas that dissipate a group's energy. We considered solutions to help leaders recognize these threats to a group's COHESION, manage tension between individual needs and group needs, and gain the perspective necessary to help teams regain focus and direction.

- **BIG HAT-LITTLE HAT** is one of the most common RIGHT VS. RIGHT dilemmas.

- **RIGHT VS. RIGHT** are the ethical dilemmas that are common sources of conflict between group members.

- **RESOLUTION PRINCIPLES** highlight three ways to resolve RIGHT VS. RIGHT dilemmas. Armed with this PRIME, leaders can help groups successfully manage ethical challenges and remain cohesive.

• Together **BLIND MEN AND THE ELEPHANT** and **LEVELS OF PERSPECTIVE** demonstrate that what looks and sounds like disagreement is often the result of individuals who are operating with different information, and who argue from their differing points of view.

Even when the dragons are under control, FRAGMENTATION within groups is natural and even expected. The PRIMES in the next chapter will help you locate the source of a group's problem and help members resolve it quickly.

> *Everyone who achieves success in a great venture solved each problem as they came to it. They helped themselves. And they were helped through powers known and unknown to them at the time they set out on their voyage. They kept going regardless of the obstacles they met.*
>
> ～   W. C. Stone

PART 3

SUMMITING

On a 14,000 foot climb in Peru, I could see that the summit was only 1,000 feet away, up the headwall.[18] The air was at its thinnest, fatigue was at its greatest, and the headwall was the steepest part of the climb. We all felt the temptation to sit down and rest, but the peak was within view and so we persevered to reach it.

Summiting[19] the mountain is what inspires every adventurer. It's the purpose for making the climb at all. It's also the hardest part of the trip. On the headwall, gravity weighs heavier, but the commitment to the outcome is absolutely clear. All available energy is focused on driving to the summit.

Near the completion of any important transformative initiative, resistant forces—the LAGGARDS—are fully organized and the danger of FRAGMENTATION is at its highest. Champions of the status quo are desperate to stop further progress. Some members of your team, whom you thought were allies, are rife with LITTLE HAT concerns. Sensing new opportunities, others members compete for attention. Some want to extend the schedule, so they'll feel better prepared, while others begin to question the purpose of the entire project.

When resistance is at its most intense, your greatest moments, your finest hours, are at hand. What you've been waiting for is actually just ahead, waiting for you. Your change effort or transformation project is almost a reality. But pay attention to the group, because your team is at its highest level of fatigue.

Groups under the stress of an arduous journey tend to break apart along predictable fault lines. The next set of five PRIMES will help you recognize early indicators of problems while you still have time to address them. They also uncover practical ways to maintain the group's COHESION.

> *New and stirring ideas are belittled, because if they are*
> *not belittled the humiliating question arises, "Why,*
> *then, are you not taking part in them?"*
>   ❧   H. G. Wells

CHAPTER 6

STRATEGIC PAUSE

Mountain climbers encounter unique challenges toward the end of their trek to the summit. The weather on a mountain can turn quickly into a blinding combination of wind and snow, known as a whiteout. With no reference point, the climber's sensation is one of floating. The way down looks the same as the way up.

Effective leaders recognize when a sense of disorientation occurs within their team. They know that something important isn't working. Whatever it is, it's time to stop everything and huddle, protect against the elements, and embrace the chaos that has embraced the team. Everyone's help is needed to figure things out and solve problems, because stakes are high.

Mountain climbers call this momentary shelter a bivouac. Universe Denters, on their quest to solve complex problems and transform organizations, call it a "Strategic Pause." Such is the Universe Denter's refuge: a time and place to think and to deal with the unexpected.

A Strategic Pause is anything but a waste of time. Although it may seem to threaten momentum, executed intentionally, this time-out can mean the difference between mere delay and utter failure. It provides a clearing for critical conversations, crucial confrontations, essential prioritizations, and vision-saving innovations.

A Strategic Pause allows people to process new information and realign with where they are (As Is), where they're going (To Be), and how they'll get there (REDPOINT). It's a time to reaffirm the team's commitment and regenerate its forward momentum. Effective leaders know when the situation calls for such a pause and how to use that time most effectively.

People tolerate a Strategic Pause differently. Some find it hard to remain still, however briefly, because no one moves forward. Others are grateful. Good leaders make the temporary halt outcome-driven and expedient. Alignment with others in a tight situation can be a wonderful experience that is intensified in a well-managed, perfectly timed Strategic Pause.

Effective leaders use this time to distinguish facts from ambient noise. They're curious about the perspectives of others and about how team members have experienced the progress made so far. Often, the information necessary to climb the last few yards is hidden in the team members themselves. The Strategic Pause creates the opportunity for the group to tap into this wisdom. Leaders understand that expectancy accompanies such a pause, because it often comes just before we put our dent in the Universe.

The four PRIMES in this section provide tools to recognize the source of misalignments. Understanding the root causes of group conflict will help you take maximum advantage of a Strategic Pause.

> *While the problems are complex and difficult to resolve*
> *... this "Strategic Pause" provides an opportunity to deal*
> *with the challenges.*
>
>   ❧   T. X. Hammes

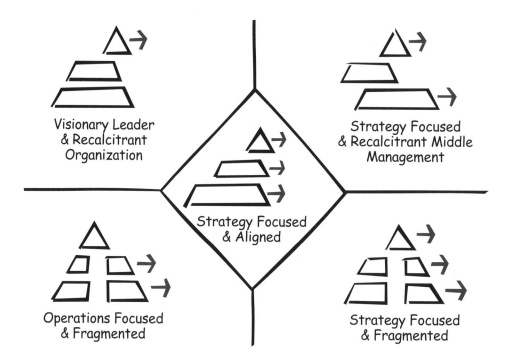

FRAGMENTATION

FRAGMENTATION

*Your team's focus and action fragment continuously,
but not all fragmentation is the same.
What kind is your team experiencing now?*

FRAGMENTATION is the splitting of will and focus among the stakeholders. A noticeable crack in the group's intentionality appears. Some question the plan, while others offer competing plans at the 11th hour. A few in the group even begin to question why the expedition was undertaken in the first place. There's no longer unity of purpose, solidarity, or commitment to the vision.

FRAGMENTATION usually happens at the worst possible time. Recognizing the beginnings of FRAGMENTATION is essential, as are timely and effective actions to reestablish COHESION.

When faced with new possibilities, people react in predictable ways. The FRAGMENTATION PRIME helps a leader visualize what kind of splintering is occurring.

Let's examine the patterns in the illustration of the FRAGMENTATION PRIME:

- The center represents the ideal condition: the leader moves out, and the team follows closely.

- The top left of the illustration shows a leader who is moving ahead, without enrolling the team. When a group finds itself alone, the vision may be lost, and the entire project could fail. The leader must rally the team.

- The bottom left section illustrates a mutiny. The leader and some of the team members at lower levels are entrenched in the status quo. They failed to internalize the STAKE, and they aren't motivated to change anything. Others take matters into their own hands and move out on their own.

- The upper right corner of the illustration shows a leader who has inspired the rank and file, but who hasn't communicated the benefits effectively to middle managers. This type of FRAGMENTATION is prevalent in government, where leaders come and go every 18 months, while career managers remain in place. If managers don't like what they hear, they adopt a "this too shall pass" attitude. Underestimating of the power of the middle team is a rookie leader's error, and a costly one.

- The most common type of FRAGMENTATION is seen at the bottom right of the illustration. In this case, the leader has rallied the team at all levels, yet some have chosen to protect the status quo. As the top moves out, the middle and bottom levels of the group split. Some move with the leader toward the vision, while others resist. This tenuous circumstance must be handled with extreme care.

There are many solutions to the problems that FRAGMENTATION creates. The PRIME that follows—LAGGARDS—offers insights about the last type of FRAGMENTATION discussed previously.

As soon as you recognize that any type of FRAGMENTATION has occurred, identify which group or groups have splintered. Use the most applicable PRIMES to bring them back into alignment, reestablish COHESION, and move forward as a unit.

Know how to listen, and you will profit even from those who talk badly.

                                                         ✌ Plutarch

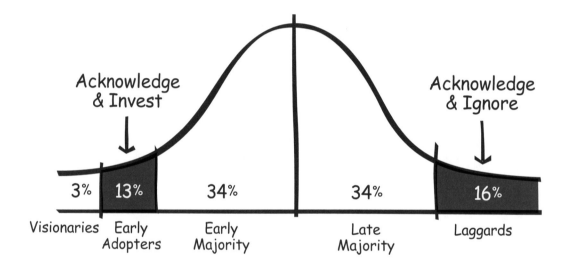

Acknowledge & Invest

Acknowledge & Ignore

3% — Visionaries
13% — Early Adopters
34% — Early Majority
34% — Late Majority
16% — Laggards

LAGGARDS

LAGGARDS

The most important people to the success of an initiative look and act much the same as the least valuable and most destructive individuals. How fast can you distinguish them?

The Innovation Adoption Curve,[20] illustrated on the previous page, shows how people react to change. Visionaries will jump at anything, but they have little credibility among other group members. Early Adopters are willing to take a risk if basic questions are answered satisfactorily. The Early Majority relies on Early Adopters for direction, while the Late Majority moves because it doesn't want to be left behind. LAGGARDS never come along; they seek only to destroy possibility by constantly asking questions, ignoring answers, and declaring why things won't work. The key for a leader is to identify the traits of individuals in a group. Effective leaders ignore the LAGGARDS and invest their time and energy in the Early Adopters.

Visionaries stand out right away. When you pursue something new, they're the ones who say, "Sure! I don't understand it, but I'm in!" They're risk junkies. They're the first to embrace new thoughts, new ideas, or new technology. It's easy to make the mistake of thinking that a visionary's enthusiasm matters, but it doesn't. Even though everyone loves to invite visionaries to parties, they'd never ask one to cover their backs. Visionaries handle risk recklessly, and everyone knows it.

Early Adopters ask important questions: "What does this new possibility mean? How is it going to affect our existing market share? What are we going to do with our existing products?" They need answers, and they listen; they want to be convinced. When Early Adopters have their questions answered satisfactorily, they say, "Okay, we don't have it all worked out yet, but we have enough information to move."

As soon as Early Adopters move, the Early Majority moves in behind them. They have their hearts in the right place and want to do what's right for the organization, but they rely on the Early Adopters as their compass.

The Late Majority wants only not to be left behind. As soon as the Early Majority moves, the Late Majority follows. Members of this group don't know how they'll be relevant, but they'll find a way because they don't want to be left out.

At first, LAGGARDS are difficult to distinguish from Early Adopters. Like Early Adopters, LAGGARDS ask great questions. They're often powerful, well prepared, and smart. Their major distinction is that they remain in place, asking more questions, even after the Early Adopters move. LAGGARDS rarely enroll fully in a Universe-denting effort. They drag their feet and often need to be carried. They love the attention. Indeed, attention-getting fuels their resistance.

A transformational leader's job was once believed to include converting LAGGARDS into the Late or Early Majorities. That belief was a trap. LAGGARDS appoint themselves as guardians of the status quo, to protect it from an uncertain and unruly future. They don't accept that they can create the future; their goal is to prevent real change or transformation at any cost.

LAGGARDS try to draw attention, to be noticed, respected, and important. They show up with "secret knowledge" and pointed questions. Trying to bring them along gives LAGGARDS the recognition they seek. Despite getting what they want, it's rare that they invest in or commit to the vision.

After years of trying to woo LAGGARDS, we've learned to ignore them. Listen to LAGGARDS along with everyone else, but as soon as they stop talking, ignore everything they said and direct your attention to the Early Adopters. Mentally banish the LAGGARDS; every hour invested in them is wasted.

Your survival and the ability to reach your goal depend on your ability to distinguish LAGGARDS from Early Adopters as quickly as possible, and pouring your energy into the latter group. When the Early Adopters move, everyone you need moves behind them. If you have 10 hours in a day, invest 11 in Early Adopters. They're your best constituency.

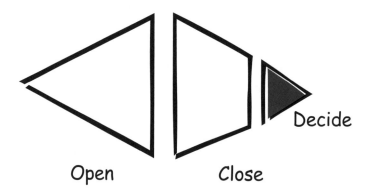

OPEN - CLOSE - DECIDE

OPEN-CLOSE-DECIDE

Regardless of how many are involved in the process, one person, at a specific moment, always makes the decision. Can you distinguish the decision maker and the decision moment?

Understanding how groups work is essential to be an effective group leader or participant. When we were building Work Group Technology at IBM— later called Web 2.0—we needed to understand natural group processes. We had teams of psychologists and behaviorists, giving us all kinds of theoretical insights. Michael Doyle and Kai Dozier stripped the challenge to essential truths, embodied in the OPEN–CLOSE–DECIDE PRIME. Once revealed, this PRIME was one I saw everywhere—from board rooms of the Fortune 500 to a group of friends on a street corner deciding where to eat lunch. Whether choosing a restaurant or a risky product launch, OPEN–CLOSE–DECIDE is at work.

Michael and Kai explained that there is an initial period of time when groups tolerate the generation of ideas (OPEN). Brainstorming is an effective technique for structuring discussion during the OPEN phase. Eventually, the group becomes less tolerant of new ideas and begins the important process of prioritization and convergence (CLOSE). Resistance turns into disregard for new ideas, while the group focuses its attention on only a few.

Finally, the group enters the third phase of the process when a choice is made (DECIDE). It's critical to recognize that the CLOSE process is distinct from the DECIDE process and both are leadership-driven. Without leaders guiding the CLOSE and DECIDE processes, groups lose momentum and get lost.

OPEN

The OPEN phase is the most fun and the easiest to lead and facilitate. It's important but frequently overvalued. The stakes are low and anything goes. Much has been written about the OPEN phase of group work, and many Web 2.0 applications support it. As long as a leader suspends judgment and makes it safe for people to offer their opinions and ideas, the primary value of the OPEN phase will be realized. Teams will generate fresh ideas; they'll build exciting concepts, and mash everything together to create innovative approaches.

CLOSE

Groups tend to enter the CLOSE phase when they run out of ideas, patience, or time. The stakes are higher than in the OPEN phase and being right becomes more important than being provocative. Convergence is more valued than divergence. The CLOSE phase is marked by a distinct tone of judgment; certain ideas are deemed worthy, and others are cast aside. Leaders must listen closely, because this is where the group begins to reveal its "decision criteria."

Decision criteria typically follow the word, "because," as in, "I don't think this is a good idea *because* it costs too much." The person who voices this statement makes it clear that he or she perceives cost as a major criterion in making a decision.

Another person might say, "I think it's a good idea. Yes, it costs more, but I still like it *because* it produces so much customer value." This speaker introduced a second criterion—"customer value"—and, at the same time, elevated its importance over cost. In the CLOSE phase, learning to distinguish criteria and their relative value is an essential skill leaders must master.

DECIDE

Like genocide, pesticide, and suicide, DECIDE is about death ("cide"). The DECIDE phase is the final act of killing off alternatives and leaving one option alive. Regardless of how many people are involved in the OPEN and CLOSE discussions, groups don't make decisions. Real decision making comes down to one person who chooses for the group.

In literally hundreds of high-stakes meetings, from banks to factories, to the halls of government and nonprofit organizations, I've learned to recognize the "DECIDE moment." Sometimes, it's barely perceptible, even to the trained eye. It happens in an instant, with a nod or a remark, made by the one person everyone is watching. In any group, one person has the power and the expectation of the others to DECIDE for all, once sufficient time and attention have been given to the OPEN and CLOSE phases.

The vote is the lone exception to the rule that one person ultimately DECIDES. The vote represents the lowest form of decision making. When collaboration fails and leadership can't be trusted, people surrender their opinions and allow math to DECIDE. Although voting is prevalent in politics, it's rarely the mechanism of choice elsewhere. The vote represents the failure of CONSENSUS; it's the process of last resort, and it's the least effective.

Some say the internet will enable new ways to generate ideas and make decisions. The internet does bring new mechanisms into the group process, and more people can be involved. OPEN–CLOSE–DECIDE endures, however, as the essential, natural group process.

Whenever you see a successful business, someone once made a courageous decision.

                                         Peter Drucker

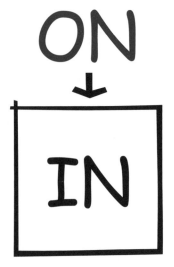

IN - ON

IN-ON

At any time, leaders are either working "in" their business or "on" their business. Where do you invest your time and attention?

The IN–ON PRIME enables leaders to distinguish between working "IN" their business from working "ON" their business. The IN–ON PRIME *will* be violated. You may be the one who violates it … often. I do. My clients do. Unless you recognize and immediately correct violations of this PRIME, any complex problem solving, change, or transformation effort will fail.

Before the IN–ON PRIME was revealed to me, my business life was full of frustration, fits and starts, and head-banging against barriers that prevented me from realizing important goals. In learning how to overcome these blockages, IN–ON became the lens through which my leadership team and I viewed our activities. As a result, the company I headed was transformed and enjoyed sustained growth.

The power of this PRIME is unleashed once you recognize that at any time, you're either working IN your business or ON your business. IN isn't ON, and there's no overlap. When working IN your business, you essentially operate it. When you work ON your business, your activities either change or transform it; you bring forth new ways for the business to operate and produce extraordinary results in the market.

Over lunch one day with my friend Kai Dosier, I said how frustrating it was that our company had not broken through the $10 million dollar revenue barrier. My team and I continually approached the target, retracted, and repeated the pattern. Everyone worked hard, and I was mystified as to why we hadn't yet succeeded. In the center of a napkin, Kai sketched the illustration on the preceding page. When he finished, Kai looked at me and said, "Leaders typically shortchange the time they devote to working ON the business." Then he asked, "Are you spending enough time working ON your business?"

Immediately, I began to distinguish my IN from my ON activities over the previous days. It became clear that I spent almost all of my time as a consultant—at work IN the business. When I helped my clients work ON their businesses, I was at work IN my own. Over the next several days, I realized where my choices had led me. Kai also turned me on to Michael Gerber's book, *The E-Myth Revisited*.[21] It further illuminated the distinction between the competing interests of IN and ON activities, but it was Kai's napkin sketch that stuck in my mind. Thanks to his insight, I saw my appointment book in a new way. Through the lens of the IN–ON PRIME, I saw what had been invisible previously, and I could no longer ignore the lopsided amount of time I allocated to work IN my business rather than ON it.

In the days that followed, I noticed that I continued to spend most of my time at work IN the business. I found that I was easily distracted from working ON my business by some shiny, bright opportunity that popped up and gave me an opportunity to run to the rescue. A client needed me; issues with the staff cried for attention; "once in a lifetime" opportunities demanded to be chased! I began to recognize that "only I can do it" and "this chance will never come again" were myths; they provided convenient excuses to avoid the relatively ambiguous responsibility of leading change; they kept me entrenched in the status quo. By working IN my business, I avoided learning how to lead and build a company. Once I began to work ON my business, and gave it the leadership attention it needed, it grew and became a terrific success story.

IN is seductive, whereas ON is ambiguous and scary. IN provides rich opportunities for leaders to take control, save the day, and earn expressions of praise and awe from staff and peers. ON carries an inherent risk of being wrong and embarrassed. IN wants all of the leader's attention and is threatened when he or she takes time to work ON the business. As long as IN keeps a leader's attention, nothing changes. Anyone can work IN a business, but if leaders don't work ON their business, neither will anyone else.

I was frustrated with my company's growth, even with the realization of the IN-ON PRIME. I saw IN pulling at me, but for the first time, I knew giving in to it would put the company's future at risk. Within a few weeks of my lunch with Kai Dosier, I asked my two top people a simple question: "What's stopping us from breaking through the $10 million revenue barrier?" They thought for a minute and then gave me a single, clear answer: as our company's leaders, we were distracted every day by the bright, shiny, seductive IN.

"Let's clear our schedules," I said. "Let's ask others to do whatever we had to do today. Let's work together until this problem is solved." We did just that and our company took off. We allocated sufficient time each week to work ON our business. We drove change and caused transformative outcomes. Later, we sold that business for tens of millions, during a sustained 35 percent growth rate.

After more than 25 years of working with many different leaders, I've concluded that failing to recognize the distinction between IN and ON—mismanaging the critical allocation of time and attention to each—is the number one reason that change and transformation efforts fail. There is no pat formula for how much energy to give IN and ON activities. Taking time to work ON the business and building this PRIME into the CULTURE, gives leaders a higher perspective to rise above the day-to-day demands.

The IN–ON PRIME may be the most important one to master in order to drive successful change and transformation, create the future, and produce extraordinary results.

IN–ON has been important, countless times, as my staff and I go about our business. We find ourselves drawing it out on scraps of paper in offices, from the marbled halls of the Nation's Capitol to the plains of Iowa and the inner cities of Kenya. IN–ON illuminates the tendency of leaders everywhere to focus their attention on one aspect of their business more than another.

The IN–ON distinction is one that every leader, change agent, and Universe Denter must recognize and master.

The four PRIMES revealed in this chapter will help you anticipate a group's need for a timely Strategic Pause and guide them through it effectively.

- **FRAGMENTATION** reveals how groups inevitably split apart, and what to do about it. Nature tends toward chaos and, while COHESION is essential, it's also unnatural. Expect FRAGMENTATION.

- **LAGGARDS** are to be ignored. Identifying LAGGARDS in any group enables you to avoid wasting time and energy. Focus your attention on the Early Adopters, who determine the group's direction and progress.

- **OPEN–CLOSE–DECIDE** reveals the process all groups go through on their way to making a decision. This PRIME enables you to perceive where the group is and where it's going. This PRIME also reveals a secret about how decisions are truly made.

- **IN–ON** illuminates where you spend your time and where you should invest more of it, to make change and transformation efforts successful. This PRIME exposes the seductive nature of working IN rather than ON your business, and makes clear its lethal attraction.

The final PRIMES in the next chapter are survival gear for truly great leaders. Outfitted with these principles, you will bypass obstacles, navigate the unexpected, and lead your teams through the rough patches every time they appear.

Choosing what you want to do, and when to do it, is an act of creation.

ൗ   Peter McWilliams

CHAPTER 7

DECLARED LEADERSHIP

The end is in sight. We've explored 28 PRIMES thus far, and once you take in the PRIMES in this final chapter, your outfitting will be complete.

Most leaders feel some sense of wanderlust. Out of the many who consider launching large-scale change and transformation initiatives, however, only a small number actually heed the call and aspire to a specific outcome. Even fewer embark on the perilous journey to step off the As Is toward the To Be. Of those who declare their vision, only a quarter of them succeed.[22]

The final four PRIMES come from this small and elite group of leaders who beat the odds. These Universe Denters are men and women with whom I have the privilege of standing, as they declare their visions of what's To Be and then do whatever it takes to bring their declared futures into existence. They understand that, in an age where collaboration, empowerment, and crowdsourcing are popular, leaders must still lead.

> *If your actions inspire others to dream more, learn more,*
> *do more, and become more, you are a leader.*
>   ꝏ John Quincy Adams

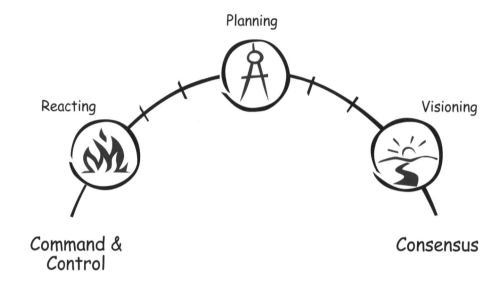

LEADERSHIP SPECTRUM

LEADERSHIP SPECTRUM

*Leaders show up to their teams in roles that range from
commanders to consensus builders.
How intentional are you about adapting your style
to the situation at hand?*

Over the years, I've observed that leaders tend to have a "default" style and a favorite decision-making process. Some are more comfortable at making command and control decisions, while others prefer to collaborate with their subordinates and peers. The most effective leaders I've observed use the LEADERSHIP SPECTRUM PRIME and are skilled at matching the decision process to each situation they encounter.

The LEADERSHIP SPECTRUM PRIME was made crystal clear to me when I had the privilege of watching a Marine Corps general in the midst of criticizing his fellow officers for overusing the command and control decision process of combat. He drew the LEADERSHIP SPECTRUM on a flip chart and told his officers, "Put four decision processes in your pocket each day. Then, decide which process is best for each situation you face."

*   **Command and Control** – Use this leadership style when the bullets start flying, when the situation is urgent, and the stakes are high. Someone has to take command and control in the heat of battle.

- **Informed Command and Control –** This leadership style works well in situations that are still urgent, but where the stakes are lower, such as when a company requires a meeting venue and reservations must be made within hours.

- **Limited Consensus –** Use this style for low-stakes strategic planning, such as the choice between competing but similar health insurance plans.

- **Consensus –** Put this in your pocket for high-stakes strategic planning and visioning, such as the creation of a five-year plan to take a new company into the marketplace.

On one end of the LEADERSHIP SPECTRUM, Command and Control is preferred when time is short and any decision made fast is better than a perfect one made too late. Outside of combat or physical emergency, use of Command and Control should be a rare occurrence.

On the other end of the LEADERSHIP SPECTRUM, Consensus is most appropriate for strategic planning, and exploring innovations and breakthrough ideas. Ineffective leaders overuse and rely on Consensus decision making, even when situations cry out for rapid Command and Control.

A leader is best when people barely know he exists.
When his work is done, his aim fulfilled, they will say:
we did it ourselves.

                                   ℘   LaoTzu

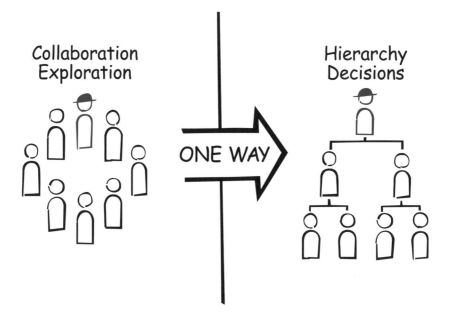

Collaboration
Exploration

Hierarchy
Decisions

ONE WAY

SHAPE SHIFTING

SHAPE SHIFTING

Leaders can assume a collaborative or an authoritarian relationship with a group but not both at once. How explicit are you about your role?

Every group needs and wants a leader. Two of the many types of leaders are characterized in this PRIME:

1. Leaders who put themselves into a collaborative relationship with their group: they roll up their sleeves, brainstorm as peers, and help formulate recommendations before the decision is made.

2. Leaders who assume a hierarchical relationship with the group and use their organizational authority to make decisions: they frequently use the Command and Control leadership style mentioned in the LEADERSHIP SPECTRUM PRIME.

Both roles are useful. The key is for leaders to be explicit about which role they take. Some decisions necessitate creativity, innovation, and the involvement and wisdom of a group. Other situations require a quick decision. The most common mistake is for leaders to declare a collaborative relationship with the group and then make authoritative decisions. This change in roles is called "SHAPE SHIFTING," and it erodes a group's trust in its leader.

In the discussion of OPEN–CLOSE–DECIDE, we learned there's no such thing as group decision making. Effective leaders understand how decisions are made and use both types of leadership described here. You must be as skilled in collaboration as you are in command and control relationships with your team. The SHAPE SHIFTING PRIME reveals potential dangers, as you navigate between these two styles.

Here's an example of a SHAPE SHIFT: A leader declares a collaborative relationship to generate ideas. Then, caught up in the spirit of the exchange, he or she suddenly shouts, "That's a terrible idea. Forget that one." Or just as destructively, "Bill, that's a great idea! We've got the budget, let's do it!" Instantly, no matter how the chairs are arranged, the process is overtaken by a hierarchy. The leader SHAPE SHIFTED and used his or her organizational authority to behave differently from everyone else. The leader valued an idea, resourced it in his or her mind, and passed judgment. The room is now a boardroom and everyone knows it. People shut down immediately and they no longer trust the process. The group becomes guarded and won't go back to collaboration. They become concerned that their ideas will be judged in public, and open them to possible embarrassment.

To avoid the often fatal mistake of SHAPE SHIFTING, you must adhere to three practices:

1. Distinguish between Collaboration with the group and a Command and Control relationship. Master the best practices of each.

2. Intentionally and explicitly choose one role or the other in any given situation.

3.   Don't shift from one role to another, if it can be avoided. If you must shift—typically from Collaboration to Command and Control— forewarn the group explicitly. Remember, it's almost impossible to return to Collaboration once the shift to Command and Control has been made.

Don't shift relationships with a group during the course of any single meeting. Collaborate with them one day, but resist the temptation to make any decisions or pass unilateral judgment on a particular idea. Collaboration typically generates recommendations, as opposed to decisions. After careful consideration of the recommendations, use your organizational authority on a later day to make a decision. Avoid SHAPE SHIFTING.

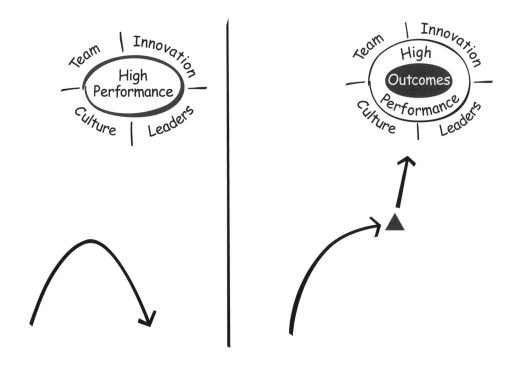

CHASE - LOSE

CHASE-LOSE

*Pursuing significant and meaningful outcomes
inspires teamwork and leadership.
Do you practice teamwork and leadership, or just talk about them?*

I've always been fascinated with high performance teams, cultures, and leaders. I've done a fair amount of team building and leadership coaching, and CHASE–LOSE revealed itself slowly over many years. This PRIME has profoundly affected how we approach problem solving, transformation, team building, and leadership development today. The CHASE–LOSE PRIME reveals three truths that appear counterintuitive:

1.   When we CHASE team, we LOSE team.

2.   When we CHASE culture, we LOSE culture.

3.   When we CHASE leadership, we LOSE leadership.

4.   When we CHASE innovation, we LOSE innovation.

This PRIME illuminates that the characteristics of a high-performance CULTURE—teamwork, innovation, leadership, and others—are not ends in themselves. Rather, they are skills and competencies gained while pursuing extraordinary outcomes.

Instead of CHASING the characteristics of high-performance CULTURE, we ought to:

1.   CHASE a meaningful outcome;

2.   Deal quickly with whatever puts that outcome at risk; build high-performance competencies in the process; and

3.   Achieve the outcomes and improve our CULTURE at the same time.

Here's an example of how the three "ought to" principles above were applied to a transformational initiative that produced extraordinary results and put a significant dent in the Universe:

> In the spring of 2001, President George W. Bush declared E-Gov—the use of the internet to transform the way government operates and delivers services—one of his top administrative priorities. The United States had slipped behind dozens of countries in its E-Gov ranking and, under the direction of Mark Forman, the federal government's Chief Information Officer at the time, our team was given the assignment to develop sweeping new E-Gov applications. The track record of projects like this was atrocious and, right away, we faced two diametrically opposed facts:
>
> 1. The biggest gains to be made required cross-government collaboration.
>
> 2. Nothing in the structure of the federal government promoted such collaboration.

At the behest of the Executive Office, we asked each agency to give us one of their best and brightest people to participate in Project Quicksilver. We gave the 75 or so who were selected a big room, computers, flip charts, coffee and juice, and a hundred days to figure out all the E-Gov projects that the United States could possibly take on. The group's task was to determine the fewest, most important projects that, with sufficient resources and leadership, could be completed in a year.

Initially, Quicksilver members were guarded and skeptical. They had seen initiatives like this come and go for years. They brainstormed and drank a lot of coffee and juice, and soon, only 73 days were left, then 51, then 39. The Quicksilver members knew their recommendations would go directly to the President's Management Council and the senior leadership of the Office of Management and Budget on the 100th day.

The group's effectiveness went up as the available time went down. Issues that put the outcome at risk—leadership, teamwork, culture—were dealt with quickly. LAGGARDS were distinguished from Early Adopters. The former were ignored, while the latter took on added responsibility as the group approached its midpoint. FRAGMENTATION within the group surfaced routinely, was quickly addressed, and recurred just as quickly. The clock kept ticking, and the stakes rose.

Then, it happened: About 70 days into the 100-day project, I entered the Quicksilver area at midmorning. Someone had brought fresh bagels and cream cheese; the place smelled of coffee ... and possibility. I noticed an amazing display of high-performance collaboration. No longer were these individuals from different government agencies; they were Quicksilver, a high-performance team, at work to solve real problems that faced our country. They met the deadline and delivered hundreds of projects to be considered, 22 of which were ultimately selected, funded, and implemented over the following year. The United States went from ranking somewhere in the 30s to number one in the world in the use of the internet to operate and deliver government services.

As program managers for the Quicksilver project, we never CHASED any direct team-building, leadership development, or innovation practices. We didn't host any workshops to facilitate CULTURE creation. We simply dealt immediately with anything that put the outcome at risk.

The CHASE–LOSE PRIME revealed itself fully on another morning in August 2007:

I served coffee to the crew that was busy putting an addition on my home for a recording studio. It was a complex project, which required carpenters, electricians, plumbers, masons, and sound engineers to collaborate and work in proximity. Moshe Nissan was in charge. An Israeli and a devout follower of the Jewish faith and traditions, he was the first to arrive every day, the last one to leave at night, and he worked his crew hard. He was a fair man and greatly admired by his teams.

The place was full of joyous noise. There was good-natured arguing, orders barked, and heavy materials carefully shaped and fastened together. More than a dozen people were at work on the site. As they came for coffee, I was struck by their diversity. There were South and Central Americans, a man from Portugal, some African Americans, a guy from the Midwest, some who identified themselves as Muslims, and a few more Jews. I commented to Moshe that his team looked like a delegation from the United Nations.

Without pausing, Moshe turned and said, "No, this is better. At the UN they just *talk* about their differences, and they *think* about collaboration. Here we work. We get along because we share work." Moshe continued, "It's *in* the work and comes *from* the work, and it *is* the work."

After reflecting on more than 25 years of experience, I agreed with Moshe.

CHASE–LOSE sets the right order to things:

- First, answer the call and step up to big challenges.

- Next, enroll others and declare your intentions with integrity.

- Then, get busy and work as quickly as possible.

- Finally, deal quickly with whatever shows up that threatens success.

The right order ensures that you have an opportunity to be part of a high-performance team, experience the profound privilege of leading powerfully, and make your dent in the Universe.

Coming together is a beginning. Keeping together is progress. Working together is success.

                                        ☙   Henry Ford

COMMITMENT VS. ATTACHMENT

COMMITMENT VS. ATTACHMENT

We can choose to "be," any way at all,
regardless of the world around us.
Are you "committed" or "attached" to your vision?

"Michael," I asked, "What's the most important thing to pay attention to in this business of creating change and transformation?"

Michael Doyle thought for a minute and said, "Taking great care of yourself, so you can persist. You have to be healthier than the whole world is sick." COMMITMENT VS. ATTACHMENT will serve you as much personally as it will in your role as a leader. This PRIME revealed itself to me in the strangest place:

> In the summer of 2008, my daughter Carli invited me to come along with her friends and my niece Katie on a road trip to Legend Valley in Ohio, to attend the Jerry Garcia Gathering in honor of the late singer and songwriter's birthday. After 10 hours spent muscling an RV across I-70, we arrived at the gate. A woman named Anna greeted us, took our tickets, and told me where to park. Anna was in her fifties, with clear blue eyes; she had long, straight, red hair, parted in the middle; and she wore a bright, flowing sundress. Anna looked like everything that was right about the 1960s.

I pulled the camper into a huge and nearly empty venue. Legend Valley could easily accommodate 100 thousand people. After the music started, the promoters reported about 200 paid attendees for the three-day event. On the second morning, I decided to give the kids some space. I sat with Anna at the gate. As a few dozen people trickled in, she and I got to talking. Anna was a mother of four and a teacher in one of the local schools. Her family was involved in promoting the event. I asked her how she could be so peaceful and relaxed in light of the fact that hardly anyone had shown up, and she and her family were going to lose some real money.

Anna explained that her family was committed to the event and had done what they could to make it available to as many people as possible. Now she was content to take what came. She had made a choice in her life to be content regardless of how the world showed up. She said, "We committed to the outcome, but we were never attached to it."

From that moment, until we pulled out of Legend Valley, I had a special time. I introduced Anna to my niece, my daughter, and her friends, and we ended up tie-dying tee shirts with the words, *"Not Attached to the Outcome,"* blazed across the back. I still wear mine with pride and fond memories.

The whole event became a time of joy, sharing, dancing, and laughing. At the end, we all chipped in, contributing to Anna and her family's expenses, and said our goodbyes reluctantly.

Anna and her family were up to something big and meaningful to them. They were wise enough to distinguish COMMITMENT from ATTACHMENT, and they created a wonderful experience for those who attended the event. They deemed their effort a success.

If our nation had been ATTACHED to the rockets that crashed instead of being COMMITTED to the outcome, John F. Kennedy's vision of a man on the Moon might never have come to pass.

Be healthier than the world is sick. Commit yourself completely to whatever calling you choose to answer. Live full out to achieve it. Take what comes and move on.

If we are always arriving and departing, it is also true that we are eternally anchored. One's destination is never a place but rather a new way of looking at things.

         Henry Miller

EPILOGUE
WANDERLUST REVISITED

What story do you tell about the challenges we face in our world today? Do you hope that someone, other than you, is busy fixing them? Do you wish they'd go away, and we could return to the "good old days?" Are you resigned to a paradigm in which the human race is spinning out of control to its ultimate destruction? Or, do you see these challenges as unprecedented invitations to live large? Do the challenges give rise to new openings? Do they encourage you to join others to achieve new levels of shared understanding about our interdependence? Do the challenges inspire you to collaborate with others to create new and transformative possibilities? Is your story one in which you're called and needed to make a meaningful contribution to a broader community? Does that calling stir within you a deep yearning to respond?

Some of us have given up the self-limiting myth that someone else is better equipped to take on the problems we face. We answer our own inner calling to become "cause agents" and put a dent in the Universe. We've seen the limits of fixing the past and we've begun to envision a transformed future. We've stepped up to contribute to our communities and to value excellence. We've made an irrevocable choice to stand for something we believe is important. We acknowledge the absence of perfect information, with faith that what we need is out there somewhere and will be made available in ways we can't predict. In that integrity, the world literally transforms.

We understand the importance of enrolling others in our vision of the future. We show up with clear declarations and incomplete plans, and ask for help to co-create the future. Many say, "Yes!" as if they have been waiting for this invitation. We begin to enroll them, first by establishing a deep and shared intimacy with the As Is conditions, and then by asking, "So what? What's at stake if we just keep doing what we're doing, and how do we benefit if our efforts succeed?" We engage in spirited dialogue, attentive to the distinctions between facts, the meanings we assign to them, the stories we tell, the beliefs we hold and let go of, and the new beliefs we take on. By making cases emotionally, analytically, and financially, we persuade ourselves and others that we'd be crazy not to seek the high ground. Something real and important is at stake. "Game on."

We know that others have made similar attempts and failed. We're wise to go slow to go fast. We assume the responsibilities intrinsic to members of an intentional community and hold ourselves accountable for whatever culture we create. We draw lines that separate behaviors we'll tolerate from those we won't. We agree neither to tolerate gossip nor to behave like victims. We refuse to talk about people in a manner that diminishes them in the eyes of the group, without a willingness to invest directly in them. We don't complain about things outside of our control. We're clear that consensus doesn't mean that everyone agrees with everything. Our decision processes will be explicit and fair. Everyone will have a chance to be heard, and we'll strive to identify the best outcomes with which we can all live. Finally, we're prepared to clean up breaches of integrity and regain our power when we fail to do what we say.

Properly outfitted, we step out. We're conscious of where we use our energy. Our only priority is to expend it to ensure that the needs of the mission and our team are met. All other expenditures of energy are avoided. We're constantly aware of our REDPOINT and we keep intermediate Redpoints in sight at all times. We anticipate problems, and we have other leaders in place to assist us. We know that, in the absence of complete information, people may become frightened or confused, which leads to resistance. We create and convey a narrative that inspires people to support the effort. We maintain a forward orientation, and close the gaps between what our plans demand and what our projections indicate. We also respect the energy it requires to maintain the unnatural state of cohesion, and we guard against losing our shared focus.

We know there are dragons. We know what many of them look like and where they hang out. We refuse to make people wrong when rights collide. We give ourselves permission to value actions that are good for the long term and the short term. We hold both justice and mercy in high regard. We want what's best for the community and for individuals. We concurrently value truth telling and loyalty to one another. We have a framework to resolve the inevitable collisions of our values. When we disagree, we're allies first; we seek to reach the same perspective and see the situation from a shared vantage point.

We know that humans plan, and the world shows up in unexpected ways. We're ready at any time to call for a Strategic Pause in the team's activities, dig in, and address issues straight-on. We recognize that the forces of FRAGMENTATION never sleep, and always work to divide the group and erode its power. We respect the influence of those in the middle of the effort, who must understand what's in it for them. Once committed, they act as powerful Sherpas,[23] who carry the largest share of the load. Others may never commit; the LAGGARDS in any group draw attention to themselves by diminishing the sense of possibility. We know how to smoke them out. We also know they want our attention only to feed their egos, so we ignore them.

We think first about what type of leader the situation demands, and we deploy those skills. In times of great peril and narrow thresholds, we're comfortable to take control and issue commands. When a situation permits, we're just as comfortable to facilitate collaborative discussions around values, aspirations, and meaning. People can trust us because we're explicit about our roles as we take them on, and when we shift from one role to another. Finally, we operate from the principle that the source of high-performance teamwork, superior leadership, meaning and purpose, shared understanding, mutual respect, and yes, even love, comes from joining with others, taking a stand with INTEGRITY, and doing good work together.

Denting the Universe feels a lot like being on top of a snow-capped peak ... and you led a team all the way. Standing on the mountain's summit, the view is more breathtaking than you imagined it could be. The air cleanses your soul. The sky is so close that you can reach up and run your fingers through it. The rest of the world disappears as you and your team stand in the reality you created together, out of the possibility you declared.

It's time to give yourself the space to appreciate fully what you've just accomplished. Let the arduous journey disappear and allow the satisfaction of denting the Universe to sink in. You broke the well of gravity and shattered the chains of the status quo. As others follow along the path you carved, they'll stand in the possibility that you and your team created. They'll take what you've established and expand its scope and depth. They'll enjoy the prospect of taking something that exists and making it bigger and better. You've given them something new to improve on, at heights never before experienced.

As you bask in the warmth of success, you think to yourself, "That was a great adventure. We learned some hard lessons and made some difficult choices." You rest, quietly appreciating the dent you and your team made in the Universe. Then you hear something. The sound is faint at first, then louder. It's a new calling, and that familiar feeling of wanderlust begins to stir inside, gently but certainly. As you peer into the distant horizon, a new possibility rises and captures your attention. It's the top of a mountain you couldn't have seen before.

Just as everything has come together and is finally settling down, the group sees you looking forward and asks, "Where are we going now?"

From the vantage point of the summit just conquered, you smile, point to a possibility made newly visible, and say, "Up there; because we can."

You're now outfitted with all of the PRIMES as we understand them today. My hope is that you hear your personal calling, respond to the stirrings of wanderlust inside you, make your declaration, and enroll others. Be intentional, persistent, and leave your dents in the Universe.

It is not the mountain we conquer but ourselves.

      Sir Edmund Hillary

NOW WHAT?

TO KNOW AND NOT TO ACT IS NOT TO KNOW

Now that you know about the PRIMES, you may wonder, "Okay, what do I do now?"

1. The first thing to do is observe. The PRIMES are already out there; they always have been and always will be. You've bumped into them for years and didn't know it.

2. Now that they've been named and distinguished, you'll recognize the PRIMES wherever you go later today or tomorrow.

3. Enjoy the speed with which the PRIMES enable you to make sense of the natural phenomena that always show up when people work together and attempt something big.

4. Share the PRIMES with others and watch them use this new vocabulary and understanding to see and alter the patterns of behavior within their groups.

Leaders have told me countless times how strange it is to see what others don't. They watch people try to make each other wrong when the argument is one of RIGHT VS. RIGHT. They witness the futility as everyone does a little about a lot of things, instead of everything about the fewest, most important things. Trust me; you too will be amazed at what you see through the lens of the PRIMES.

When you look at the world through the distinctions of the PRIMES, you'll discover that the principles embodied in the PRIMES are expressed in the stuff that happens when people work together. As your skills grow in identifying and using the insights of the PRIMES, you'll be emboldened and you may even feel restless.

Get in touch with your calling. Our world is a "target-rich" environment. It's pleading for you to activate, engage, and take a stand for something. Listen and commit to something (with INTEGRITY), or recommit to something with which you are already involved.

Help others to distinguish the PRIMES. Although I'd love it, not everyone will take the time to read this book. Just as the PRIMES were revealed to me, one by one and just in time, you have an opportunity to reveal each PRIME as it shows up in the groups you work with or lead.

Know that you're not alone. You'll find resources and support at www.theprimes.com. Veteran Universe Denters also "meet" at The Clearing (www.theclearing.com). We're involved in major transformation efforts throughout the world today. When you're up to something really big, we're prepared to partner with you to achieve your vision and produce extraordinary results.

Take your stand and the Universe will surprise you by how much it's ready to help.

NOTES

PROLOGUE

1.   Howard Gardner, *Responsibility at Work* (San Francisco: Jossey-Bass, 2007).

CHAPTER 1

2.   Russell L. Ackoff, *Creating the Corporate Future* (New York: John Wiley & Sons, 1981). Dr. Ackoff looks deeply into the study of transformation. He calls those who engage in this type of planning, "interactivists." They ascribe to the belief that, "The future is largely subject to creation." Dr. Ackoff primarily focuses on system-level transformation. On an individual level, the concept of transformation has also been proffered by many writers within the self-help and human potential movement, most notably by Carl Rogers, Alan Watts, Fernando Flores, Abraham Maslow, Werner Erhart, Victor Frankl, and Alexander Everett.

3.   James MacGregor Burns, *Transforming Leadership* (New York: Grove Press, 2003). This book presents case studies of leaders who took up the mantle to lead large-scale transformation activities. Burns explores the difference between change and transformation in the second chapter, which he opens with the statement, "Of all the tasks on the work agenda of leadership analysis, first and foremost is an understanding of human change, because its nature is the key to the rest."

4.   John F. Kennedy, "Special Message to the Congress on Urgent National Needs." Delivered in person before a joint session of Congress, Washington, D.C., May 25, 1961. (Boston: Archives, John F. Kennedy Presidential Library & Museum).

5.   Total Quality Management (TQM): A set of management practices throughout the organization, geared to ensure the organization consistently meets or exceeds customer requirements. TQM places strong focus on process measurement and controls as means of continuous improvement.

6. Activity Based Costing (ABC): An accounting technique used to determine the costs associated with the manufacture and sale of a product or service that does not take the organizational structure of the company into account.

7. Six Sigma: A rigorous and disciplined methodology that uses data and statistical analysis to measure and improve a company's operational performance by identifying and eliminating defects.

8. Jeffrey Conklin, *Dialogue Mapping: Building Shared Understanding of Wicked Problems* (West Sussex, England: John Wiley & Sons, Ltd., 1981). Jeff Conklin's book delves into the world of "wicked problems" (as opposed to tame problems) and how to solve them. Jeff is one of the leading experts on the social process of solving wicked problems, which he defines as having the following six characteristics:

    a. You don't understand the problem until you develop a solution. Every solution offered exposes new aspects of the problem and requires further adjustments. There's no definitive statement of the problem. Wicked problems are ill-structured and feature an evolving set of interlocking issues and constraints.

    b. There's no "stopping rule." Since there's no definitive "the problem," there's also no definitive "the solution."

        The problem-solving process ends when resources such as time, money, or energy are depleted; not when an optimal solution emerges.

    c. Solutions are not right or wrong; they're simply "better/worse" or "good enough/not good enough." To determine the quality of solutions isn't objective and can't be derived from following a formula.

    d. Each wicked problem is unique, and the solution will always be custom designed and fitted. Over time we may acquire wisdom and experience about approaches to wicked problems, but we're always beginners as we approach a new problem.

    e. Every solution is a "one-shot operation." Every attempt has consequences. This is the "Catch 22" of wicked problems: you can't learn about the problem without trying solutions, but every solution is expensive and has lasting consequences that may spawn new wicked problems.

f.   There's no given alternative solution. A host of potential solutions may be developed, but others are never imagined. To devise potential solutions is a creative process. To determine which solutions should be pursued and implemented is a matter of judgment.

9.   www.DevelopmentMarketplace.org.

10.   www.GlobalGiving.org.

11.   James MacGregor Burn, *Transforming Leadership* (New York: Grove Press, 2003) 166.

CHAPTER 2

12.   Martin Luther King, Jr., "I Have a Dream," March on Washington, D.C., August 28, 1963.

CHAPTER 3

13.   Jeffrey Conklin, *Dialogue Mapping: Building Shared Understanding of Wicked Problems* (West Sussex, England: John Wiley & Sons, Ltd., 1981).

CHAPTER 4

14.   ZDNet.com, January 2009. This study reported that 68 percent of IT projects fail. There are many sources and reports available on the Internet for failure rates of enterprise projects.

15.   John Kelly, Colin Cook, and Dan Spitzer, *Unlocking Shareholder Value, the Keys to Success* (KPMG, 1999).

CHAPTER 5

16.   Here be Dragons: That English mapmakers formerly placed the phrase "here be dragons" at the edges of their known world has somehow become general knowledge.

17.   Kidder, Rushworth M. Institute for Global Ethics.
      Reference all of Rush's books at www.globalethics.org. I strongly encourage

you to become familiar with the Institute and Dr. Kidder's books, especially *How Good People Make Tough Choices* (New York: Fireside, 1995) and *Moral Courage* (New York: HarperCollins, 2005).

PART 3

18. Headwall: A steep slope or precipice rising at the head of a valley or glacial cirque.

19. Summiting: To climb to the summit of a mountain.

CHAPTER 6

20. Everett M. Rogers, *Diffusion of Innovation* (New York: Free Press, 1962). Everett Rogers first introduced the "Innovation Adoption Curve" in 1962, as a way to explain how corn farmers in Iowa adopted or resisted new technologies. He quantified laggards as about 16 percent of any given system. In 1991, Geoffrey Moore used the same idea in his book, *Crossing the Chasm* (HarperCollins Publishers, Inc., New York, 1991, 1999, 2002). Moore illustrated how high-tech innovations were being adopted by the markets during the Internet expansion. Both authors provide relevant insights for today's Universe Denters.

21. Michael E. Gerber, *The E-Myth Revisited* (New York: HarperCollins Publishers, Inc., 2001).

CHAPTER 7

22. ZDNet.com.

EPILOGUE

23. Sherpa: A member of a Tibetan people living on the high southern slopes of the Himalayas in eastern Nepal and known for providing support for foreign trekkers and mountain climbers.

INDEX OF THE PRIMES
(alphabetical)

ABOUT THE AUTHOR

CHRIS McGOFF

As Founder of The Clearing Inc., **www.theclearing.com**, a Washington, DC-based strategic management consulting firm, Chris is recognized worldwide as an expert in the field of complex problem solving and organizational transformation. Facilitating strategy sessions for more than 10,000 government and industry professionals, Chris has developed a uniquely effective approach to help drive high-stakes change and innovation efforts for over 25 years. His clients include the World Bank, United Nations, AARP, DuPont, IBM, Boeing, Consol Energy, the U.S. Department of Defense and most of the other U.S. federal agencies and departments. Chris is also a professor at the University of Maryland Graduate School of Public Policy. Chris and his wife, Claire, live in the Washington, D.C. area with their six children.

Now Chris McGoff shares 32 bite-size chunks of solid wisdom and proven expertise - *The PRIMES*. His book illuminates the way forward for 21st century problem solvers and Universe Denters. For more information about Chris McGoff and to learn how to apply the PRIMES, visit **www.thePRIMES.com**.